Doing Interviews

Doing Interviews (by Steiner Kvale) is the second part of *The SAGE Qualitative Research Kit*. This *Kit* comprises eight books and taken together the *Kit* represents the most extensive and detailed introduction to the process of doing qualitative research. This book can be used in conjunction with other titles in the *Kit* as part of this overall introduction to qualitative methods but this book can equally well be used on its own as introduction to doing interviews.

Complete list of titles in *The SAGE Qualitative Research Kit*

- Designing Qualitative Research *Uwe Flick*
- Doing Interviews *Steinar Kvale*
- Doing Ethnographic and Observational Research *Michael Angrosino*
- Doing Focus Groups *Rosaline Barbour*
- Using Visual Data in Qualitative Research *Marcus Banks*
- Analysing Qualitative Data *Graham R. Gibbs*
- Doing Conversation, Discourse and Document Analysis *Tim Rapley*
- Managing Quality in Qualitative Research *Uwe Flick*

Members of the Editorial Advisory Board

Doing Interviews

Steinar Kvale

SAGE

Los Angeles • London • New Delhi • Singapore

First published 2007
Reprinted 2008

 SAGE Publications Ltd
1 Oliver's Yard
55 City Road
London EC1Y 1SP

SAGE Publications Inc.
2455 Teller Road
Thousand Oaks, California 91320

SAGE Publications India Pvt Ltd
B 1/I 1 Mohan Cooperative Industrial Area
Mathura Road, New Delhi 110 044
India

SAGE Publications Asia-Pacific Pte Ltd
33 Pekin Street #02-01
Far East Square
Singapore 048763

Library of Congress Control Number: 2006938284

British Library Cataloguing in Publication data

A catalogue record for this book is available from the British Library

ISBN 978-0-7619-4977-0

Typeset by C&M Digitals (P) Ltd, Chennai, India
Printed in Great Britain by The Cromwell Press Ltd, Trowbridge, Wiltshire
Printed on paper from sustainable resources

▌▌ Contents

List of illustrations		vii
Editorial introduction (Uwe Flick)		ix
About this book (Uwe Flick)		xv
Preface		xvii
Acknowledgements		xxi
1	Introduction to interview research	1
2	Epistemological issues of interviewing	10
3	Ethical issues of interviewing	23
4	Planning an interview study	33
5	Conducting an interview	51
6	Interview variations	67
7	Interview quality	98
8	Transcribing interviews	92
9	Analyzing interviews	101
10	Validation and generalization of interview knowledge	120
11	Reporting interview knowledge	129
12	Enhancing interview quality	136
	Glossary	146
	References	150
	Author index	155
	Subject index	157

▐▌ List of illustrations

Boxes

1.1   An interview on grading   2
1.2   An interview on team work   3
1.3   An interview with two young men   3
2.1   Power asymmetry in qualitative research interviews   14
2.2   A philosophical dialogue on love   16
2.3   A therapeutic interview on hate   17
3.1   Ethical issues at seven research stages   24
3.2   Ethical questions at the start of an interview study   26
4.1   Emotional dynamics of an interview journey   34
4.2   Seven stages of an interview inquiry   35
4.3   Seven stages of a grade study   36
5.1   Demonstration interview   52
5.2   Interview questions   60
5.3   Linguistic forms of questions   63
5.4   Second questions   64
6.1   Piaget's interview about a child's dreams   69
6.2   A craftsman's narrative   73
6.3   An active challenging interview   76
7.1   Hamlet's interview   79
7.2   Quality criteria for an interview   80
7.3   Interviewer qualifications   81
7.4   Crossing interview discourses   83
7.5   Standard criticisms of qualitative interviews   84
8.1   Transcription for conversation analysis   96
9.1   Six steps of analysis   102
9.2   Ad hoc techniques of interview analysis   116
11.1 Investigating with the final report in mind   131
12.1 Learning interviewing by transcribing interviews   137
12.2 An interview practicum   138
12.3 Internal criticisms of interview research   140

Figure

9.1   Categorization of teacher–pupil relationship   106

Tables

4.1   From interview statements to questionnaire items   45
5.1   Research questions and interview questions   59
9.1   Modes of interview analysis   104
9.2   Meaning condensation   108
10.1 Contexts of interpretation and communities of validation   125

Editorial introduction
Uwe Flick

- Introduction to *The SAGE Qualitative Research Kit*
- What is qualitative research?
- How do we conduct qualitative research?
- Scope of *The SAGE Qualitative Research Kit*

Introduction to *The SAGE Qualitative Research Kit*

In recent years, qualitative research has enjoyed a period of unprecedented growth and diversification as it has become an established and respected research approach across a variety of disciplines and contexts. An increasing number of students, teachers and practitioners are facing questions and problems of how to do qualitative research – in general and for their specific individual purposes. To answer these questions, and to address such practical problems on a how-to-do level, is the main purpose of *The SAGE Qualitative Research Kit*.

The books in *The SAGE Qualitative Research Kit* collectively address the core issues that arise when we actually do qualitative research. Each book focuses on key methods (e.g. interviews or focus groups) or materials (e.g. visual data or discourse) that are used for studying the social world in qualitative terms. Moreover, the books in the *Kit* have been written with the needs of many different types of reader in mind. As such, the *Kit* and the individual books will be of use to a wide variety of users:

- *Practitioners* of qualitative research in the social sciences, medical research, marketing research, evaluation, organizational, business and management studies, cognitive science, etc., who face the problem of planning and conducting a specific study using qualitative methods.
- *University teachers* and lecturers in these fields using qualitative methods will be expected to use these series as a basis of their teaching.

- *Undergraduate and graduate students* of social sciences, nursing, education, psychology and other fields where qualitative methods are a (main) part of the university training including practical applications (e.g. for writing a thesis).

Each book in *The SAGE Qualitative Research Kit* has been written by a distinguished author with extensive experience in their field and in the practice with methods they write about. When reading the whole series of books from the beginning to the end, you will repeatedly come across some issues which are central to any sort of qualitative research – such as ethics, designing research or assessing quality. However, in each book such issues are addressed from the specific methodological angle of the authors and the approach they describe. Thus you may find different approaches to issues of quality or different suggestions of how to analyze qualitative data in the different books, which will combine to present a comprehensive picture of the field as a whole.

What is qualitative research?

It has become more and more difficult to find a common definition of qualitative research which is accepted by the majority of qualitative research approaches and researchers. Qualitative research is no longer just simply '*not* quantitative research', but has developed an identity (or maybe multiple identities) of its own.

Despite the multiplicity of approaches to qualitative research, some common features of qualitative research can be identified. Qualitative research is intended to approach the world 'out there' (not in specialized research settings such as laboratories) and to understand, describe and sometimes explain social phenomena 'from the inside' in a number of different ways:

- By analyzing experiences of individuals or groups. Experiences can be related to biographical life histories or to (everyday or professional) practices; they may be addressed by analyzing everyday knowledge, accounts and stories.
- By analyzing interactions and communications in the making. This can be based on observing or recording practices of interacting and communicating and analyzing this material.
- By analyzing documents (texts, images, film or music) or similar traces of experiences or interactions.

Common to such approaches is that they seek to unpick how people construct the world around them, what they are doing or what is happening to them in terms that are meaningful and that offer rich insight. Interactions and documents are seen as ways of constituting social processes and artefacts collaboratively (or conflictingly). All of these approaches represent ways of meaning, which can be reconstructed and analyzed with different qualitative methods that allow the researcher to develop (more or less generalizable) models, typologies, theories as ways of describing and explaining social (or psychological) issues.

How do we conduct qualitative research?

Can we identify common ways of doing qualitative research if we take into account that there are different theoretical, epistemological and methodological approaches to qualitative research and that the issues that are studied are very diverse as well? We can at least identify some common features of how qualitative research is done.

- Qualitative researchers are interested in accessing experiences, interactions and documents in their natural context and in a way that gives room to the particularities of them and the materials in which they are studied.
- Qualitative research refrains from setting up a well-defined concept of what is studied and from formulating hypotheses in the beginning in order to test them. Rather, concepts (or hypotheses, if they are used) are developed and refined in the process of research.
- Qualitative research starts from the idea that methods and theories should be appropriate to what is studied. If the existing methods do not fit to a concrete issue or field, they are adapted or new methods or approaches are developed.
- Researchers themselves are an important part of the research process, either in terms of their own personal presence as researchers, or in terms of their experiences in the field and with the reflexivity they bring to the role – as are members of the field under study.
- Qualitative research takes context and cases seriously for understanding an issue under study. A lot of qualitative research is based on case studies or a series of case studies, and often the case (its history and complexity) is an important context for understanding what is studied.
- A major part of qualitative research is based on text and writing – from field notes and transcripts to descriptions and interpretations and finally to the presentation of the findings and of the research as a whole. Therefore, issues of transforming complex social situations (or other materials such as images) into texts – issues of transcribing and writing in general – are major concerns of qualitative research.
- If methods are supposed to be adequate to what is under study, approaches to defining and assessing the quality of qualitative research (still) have to be discussed in specific ways that are appropriate for qualitative research and even for specific approaches in qualitative research.

Scope of *The SAGE Qualitative Research Kit*

- *Designing Qualitative Research* (Uwe Flick) gives a brief introduction to qualitative research from the point of view of how to plan and design a concrete study using qualitative research in one way or the other. It is intended to outline a framework for the other books in *The Sage Qualitative Research Kit* by focusing on how-to-do problems and on how to solve such problems in the research process. The book will address issues of constructing a research design in qualitative research; it will outline stepping-stones in making a research project work and will discuss practical problems such as resources in qualitative research but also more methodological issues like quality of qualitative research and also ethics. This framework is spelled out in more details in the other books in the *Kit*.
- Three books are devoted to collecting or producing data in qualitative research. They take up the issues briefly outlined in the first book and approach them in a much more detailed and focused way for the specific method. First, *Doing Interviews* (Steinar Kvale) addresses the theoretical, epistemological, ethical and practical issues of interviewing people about specific issues or their life history. *Doing Ethnographic and Observational Research* (Michael Angrosino) focuses on the second major approach to collecting and producing qualitative data. Here again practical issues (like selecting sites, methods of collecting data in ethnography, special problems of analyzing them) are discussed in the context of more general issues (ethics, representations, quality and adequacy of ethnography as an approach). In *Doing Focus Groups* (Rosaline Barbour) the third of the most important qualitative methods of producing data is presented. Here again we find a strong focus on how-to-do issues of sampling, designing and analyzing the data and on how to produce them in focus groups.
- Three further volumes are devoted to analyzing specific types of qualitative data. *Using Visual Data in Qualitative Research* (Marcus Banks) extends the focus to the third type of qualitative data (beyond verbal data coming from interviews and focus groups and observational data). The use of visual data has not only become a major trend in social research in general, but confronts researchers with new practical problems in using them and analyzing them and produces new ethical issues. In *Analyzing Qualitative Data* (Graham R. Gibbs), several practical approaches and issues of making sense of any sort of qualitative data are addressed. Special attention is paid to practices of coding, of comparing and of using computer-assisted qualitative data analysis. Here, the focus is on verbal data like interviews, focus groups or biographies. *Doing Conversation, Discourse and Document Analysis* (Tim Rapley) extends this focus to different types of data, relevant for analyzing discourses. Here, the focus is on existing material (like documents) and on recording everyday

conversations and on finding traces of discourses. Practical issues such as generating an archive, transcribing video materials and of how to analyze discourses with such types of data are discussed.

- *Managing Quality in Qualitative Research* (Uwe Flick) takes up the issue of quality in qualitative research, which has been briefly addressed in specific contexts in other books in the *Kit*, in a more general way. Here, quality is looked at from the angle of using or reformulating existing or defining new criteria for qualitative research. This book will examine the ongoing debates about what should count as defining 'quality' and validity in qualitative methodologies and will examine the many strategies for promoting and managing quality in qualitative research. Special attention is paid to the strategy of triangulation in qualitative research and to the use of quantitative research in the context of promoting the quality of qualitative research.

Before I go on to outline the focus of this book and its role in the *Kit*, I would like to thank some people at SAGE who were important in making this *Kit* happen. Michael Carmichael suggested this project to me some time ago and was very helpful with his suggestions in the beginning. Patrick Brindle took over and continued this support, as did Vanessa Harwood and Jeremy Toynbee in making books out of the manuscripts we provided.

About this book
Uwe Flick

Interviews are one of the major approaches in collecting data in qualitative research. We know a variety of ways of how to do interviews with different aims and principles. At the same time, interviewing comes along with a number of advantages, practices and problems common to all the alternatives of doing interviews. We can address doing interviews on different levels – theoretically, epistemologically, ethically and practically. Once an interview has been done, several steps follow: specific ways of documenting what happened in the single interview lead to needs and rules for transcription. Interview data demand specific ways of performing qualitative analysis. Doing interviews comes with specific needs of increasing the interview quality in general and its validity in particular and finally of reporting what was said and how it was analyzed.

This book addresses all these issues for doing interviews in great detail and is based on the author's long experience of doing interviews and writing about interviews and interviewing. This book is a part of *The SAGE Qualitative Research Kit* and has a strong focus on collecting data but also on specific issues of analyzing and evaluating this specific form of data. Therefore some of the other books in *The SAGE Qualitative Research Kit* should be helpful in complementing what is said in this book. In particular, the books of Gibbs (2007) on analyzing qualitative data and Rapley (2007) on discourse and conversation analysis give more information on how to analyze qualitative data from interviews (and other sources). The book of Flick (2007a) goes more into the details of planning and designing qualitative research (and of doing interviews) in general. Issues of quality in qualitative research, which are also the subject of this book, are discussed in more detail in the book on managing quality in qualitative research by Flick (2007b). Alternative or additional ways of collecting data are outlined in the other books of *The SAGE Qualitative Research Kit*: Angrosino (2007) introduces participant observation and ethnography (and the use of interviews in this context also). Barbour (2007) goes more into details about focus groups as an alternative to single interviews and Banks (2007) addresses the use of visual data in more detail.

▌▌ Preface

Aims of the book

Interview research is a craft, which is learned through practising interviewing. This book prepares for learning interviewing in practice, it addresses hands-on issues of how to carry out an interview inquiry, from its inception to the final report, providing examples and guidelines along the way. Furthermore, it provides conceptual frames for understanding research interviewing and addresses epistemological and ethical issues raised by qualitative interview research.

A qualitative research interview attempts to understand the world from the subjects' points of view, to unfold the meaning of peoples' experiences, to uncover their lived world prior to scientific explanations. This book seeks to lay out the richness and the scope of qualitative interviews in social science research. There will be an emphasis on the pragmatic use-value of interview-produced knowledge and on the ethical issues that are raised by using interview conversations for research purposes.

The interview is a specific form of conversation where knowledge is produced through the interaction between an interviewer and an interviewee. The research interview will be compared to other forms of conversation such as philosophical dialogues and psychotherapeutic interviews. Different types of research interviews are described, such as narrative interviews, factual interviews, focus group interviews and confrontational interviews. The live interview conversation is one stage of a larger research process. An interview inquiry includes pre-interview stages of thematic clarification of the research topic and the designing of the research project. Furthermore, there are the post-interview stages of transcription, analysis, verification and reporting of the interview findings.

The systematic application of qualitative interviews is relatively new in the social sciences, and to some extent also controversial. Epistemological issues of using conversations for research purposes will be treated in relation to traditional and newer conceptions of knowledge. Throughout the book it will be pointed out how many of the practical issues to be decided throughout an interview inquiry are embedded in epistemological presuppositions and have ethical consequences. Such concerns range from the validity of leading questions to ethical concerns of interviewing about private issues for public reading.

Structure of the book

The craft of interviewing is learned by practising interviewing and not by reading a book. However, accumulated experiences from research interviewing may be presented in a book form, with examples from interviews and with suggested guidelines as condensed summaries from interview practice. In this book I pass on experiences gained from interview practice and guidelines drawn out from these experiences – my own, my students' and those of others reported in the interview literature. In lieu of actual practice with interviewing, examples are given from interviews to introduce some of the many practical and conceptual issues raised by using conversations for research purposes. The chapters will take issue with the apparently mystical skills of the interview craft, break them down in discrete steps, give examples, and point out the technical, conceptual and ethical issues involved.

The first chapter gives some examples from research interviews and provides a brief historical overview of the use of research interviews. The next two chapters address epistemological and ethical issues raised by using conversations for research purposes. The following chapters then, on a practical level, take the reader through seven stages of an interview investigation – starting with the pre-interview stages of thematizing the research topic and formulating the purpose of the study, and thereafter the designing of the entire interview investigation. The interview situation is dealt with in three chapters on how to conduct a semi-structured life-world interview, on varieties of interview types and on interview quality. Thereafter the post-interview stages of transcribing, analyzing, validation and generalization, and reporting are treated.

Focus of the book

The main focus in this book will be on interviewing, and the pre- and post-interviewing stages are primarily treated with respect to implications for the interview situation. Throughout the book the interrelatedness of the different stages of an interview inquiry is emphasized. I repeatedly point out how decisions at one stage of an interview investigation open or close options at other stages; the researcher is thus recommended to have the entire research process in mind during the different stages of the interview journey.

In the following chapters I shall attempt to steer between the Scylla of rigid objective structures in an all-method approach and the Charybdis of free subjective spontaneity in a no-method approach, by focusing on the expertise, skills and craftsmanship of the interviewer. Interviewing is a craft to be learned through practising interviewing, ideally through apprenticeship within a community of practice with experienced interview researchers. The learning goal of the book is to prepare the reader for learning research interviewing by exercising interviewing, and to provide conceptual frameworks for reflecting upon interview practice and the knowledge it produces. After reading the book, students should be conceptually prepared to answer questions about their interview study such as:

- How to conceive of epistemological issues of interview research (Chapter 2).
- How to address ethical issues of interviewing (Chapter 3).
- How to design an interview study (Chapter 4).
- How to plan and carry out a research interview (Chapter 5).
- How to choose among the varieties of interview types (Chapter 6).
- How to evaluate the quality of an interview (Chapter 7).
- How to transcribe an interview (Chapter 8).
- How to analyze an interview (Chapter 9).
- How to verify interview knowledge (Chapter 10).
- How to report an interview (Chapter 11).

Exercise for starting to learn interviewing

Readers who want to learn interviewing the way a craft is learned, should stop reading the book now, or at the latest after the first three introductory conceptual chapters, and perform the following task:

Obtain about three tape-recorded research interviews, spend a week transcribing them, and reflecting on the processes and problems of transcribing and interviewing.

After this hands-on experience the learners may start reading the practical how-to-do suggestions of this book. Most likely, they will then discover that through their own practice they have already learned much of what is written on the following pages. Some of the expected learning lessons are listed in Box 12.1, 'Learning Interviewing by Transcribing Interviews', in the final chapter of this book.

Readers who choose to continue reading the book without the transcription exercise are strongly recommended to practice interviewing in pilot studies, and ideally through apprenticeship learning in interview projects of experienced researchers, before embarking on a full-size interview project of their own.

▌▌ Acknowledgements

This book treats the practice of research interviewing. It is based on my more extensive book "*InterViews–an Introduction to Qualitative Research Interviewing*" from 1996. The present book is shorter, more focused on the practical how-to-do aspects of research interviewing, and it draws in more recent literature. It goes beyond the earlier focus on empathetic consensual interviews and also discusses active confrontational interviews. In addition to overviews of interview analysis focusing on meaning, this book includes interview analyses focusing on language. The present book also puts stronger emphasis on the consequences of understanding interviewing as a craft for learning interviewing.

The book is based on conducting, teaching and supervising interview research, with inspiration from my students and from Torben K. Jensen, my co-teacher of interview courses. In the preparation of this manuscript I have received valuable comments from in particular Egill Hedinn Bragason, Svend Brinkmann, Pernille Dohn, Morten Novrup Henriksen, Berit Lassesen, Philipp Höhl and my wife Tone Saugstad. I am also grateful to my secretary Lone Hansen, who again has managed to keep the many re-workings of the manuscript together.

Steinar Kvale

1
Introduction to interview research

Three interview sequences   1
Interview research in history and in the social sciences   5
Methodological and ethical issues   7

Chapter objectives
After reading this chapter you should

- be familiar with some examples of research interviews;
- know about interview research in a historical and social context; and
- understand methodological and ethical issues related to interviewing.

Three interview sequences

If you want to know how people understand their world and their lives, why not talk with them? Conversation is a basic mode of human interaction. Human beings talk with each other, they interact, pose questions and answer questions. Through conversations we get to know other people, get to learn about their experiences, feelings and hopes and the world they live in. In an interview conversation, the researcher asks about, and listens to, what people themselves tell about their lived world, about their dreams, fears and hopes, hears their views and opinions in their own words, and learns about their school and work situation, their family and social life. The research interview is an inter-view where knowledge is constructed in the inter-action between the interviewer and the interviewee.

Below follow interview sequences from three research projects, treating Danish pupils' views on grading in high school in Denmark, Canadian teachers' views on their work situation in a postmodern society, and the views of the downtrodden on their living conditions in a French suburb, respectively.

The passages serve here to give a first impression of what a qualitative research interview may look like, and they will be returned to throughout the book in discussions of interviewing and of analyzing interviews.

Box 1.1   An interview on grading

Interviewer: You mentioned previously something about grades, would you please try and say more about that?

Pupil: Grades are often unjust, because very often – very often – they are only a measure of how much you talk, and how much you agree with the teacher's opinion. For instance, I may state an opinion on the basis of a tested ideology, and which is against the teacher's ideology. The teacher will then, because it is his ideology, which he finds to be the best one, of course say that what he is saying is right and what I am saying is wrong.

Interviewer: How should that influence the grade?

Pupil: Well, because he would then think that I was an idiot – who comes up with the wrong answers.

Interviewer: Is this not only your postulate?

Pupil: No, there are lots of concrete examples.

The first interview sequence (Box 1.1) is taken from a study I conducted on the effects of grading in Danish high schools, and was conducted by one of my students. The overall design of the study is presented later (Box 4.3). Here we see how the pupil, in a response to an open question from the interviewer, himself introduces an important dimension of his experience of grades – they are unfair – and then spontaneously gives several reasons why they are unfair. The interviewer critically follows up the answers, asks for specifics, and tests the strength of the pupil's belief through counter-questions where he doubts what the pupil tells him. This rather simple form of straightforward questioning contrasts with the reciprocity of everyday conversations. The interviewer is in a power position and sets the stage by determining the topic of the interchange; it is the interviewer who asks and the interviewee who answers. The researcher does not contribute with his position on the issue, nor does the pupil ask the interviewer about his view of grades.

The next sequence (Box 1.2) is from Hargreaves's study of the work situation of Canadian teachers with changes of forms of school leadership in a postmodern society. Hargreaves interviewed Canadian teachers about their work situation in the transit from a modern to a postmodern age. One key theme that emerged was the tension between individualism and collegiality. The teacher quoted in Box 1.2 is thus rather critical of the school administration's requirements of teamwork, which he regards as a control counteracting creative teaching by the individual teachers. The interviewer does not merely register opinions, but is also asking for elaborations, and receives the teacher's arguments for why he does not think that anybody should have to participate in the form of teamwork he is subjected to. Hargreaves interpreted this and other interview sequences on team work as expressions of a 'contrived collegiality' (see chapter 9 in the present book.

Box 1.2   An interview on team work

Teacher: It's being encouraged more and more. They've been through all the schools. They want you working as a team.

Interviewer: Do you think that's good?

Teacher: So long as they allow for the creativity of the individual to modify the program. But if they want everything lock-stepped, identical – no, I think it would be disastrous, because you're going to get some people that won't think at all, that just sit back and coast on somebody else's brains and I don't feel that's good for anybody.

Interviewer: Do you feel you're given that space at the moment?

Teacher: With (my teaching partner) I am. I know with some others here, I wouldn't ... I'd go crazy.

Interviewer: How would that be ...?

Teacher: Basically controlled. They would want – first of all it would be their ideas. And I would have to fit into their teaching style, and it would have to fit into their time slot. And I don't think anybody should have to work like that.

Source: Hargreaves (1994, pp. 178–9).

The next sequence (Box 1.3 overleaf) is from a large interview project on the conditions of the downtrodden by the French sociologist Bourdieu and his co-workers. The sequence in Box 1.3 is taken from one of the many interviews reported at length by Bourdieu et al. in their book on the situation of the immigrants and the poor in France. The two young men in the interview sequence in Box 1.3 are living in a suburban housing project in the north of France under dismal living conditions (when editing the present book in late 2005, there were in France large uprisings among the youth in these suburbs, protesting against their miserable situation and harassment by the police). In the interview more than a decade earlier Bourdieu is not a neutral questioner, but expresses his own attitudes and feelings towards the situation of the young men, as well as taking a critical attitude towards their account.

Box 1.3 An interview with two young men

- You were telling me that it wasn't much fun around here, why? What is it, your job, your leisure time?

François: Yeah, both work and leisure. Even in this neighborhood there is nothing much.

Ali: There's no leisure activities.

François: We have this leisure center but the neighbors complain.

Ali: They're not very nice, that's true.

- why do they complain, because they....

François: Because we hang around the public garden, and in the evening here is nothing in our project, we have to go in the hallways when it's too cold outside. And when there's too much noise and stuff, they call the cops.

(...)

- You are not telling me the whole story....

Ali: We are always getting assaulted in our project; just yesterday we got some tear gas thrown at us, really, by a guy in an apartment. A bodybuilder. A pumper.

- Why, what were you doing, bugging him?

François: No, when we are in the entryway he lives just above, when we are in the hall we talk, sometimes we shout.

- But that took place during the daytime, at night?

François: No, just in the evening.

- Late?

François: Late, around 10, 11 o'clock.

- Well you know, he's got the right to snooze. The tear gas is a bit much but if you got on his nerves all night, you can see where he's coming from, right?

Ali: Yeah, but he could just come down and say. ...

- Yes, sure, he could come down and merely say 'go somewhere else'. ...

Ali: Instead of tear gas.

Source: Bourdieu et al. (1999, pp. 64-5).

These three interviews address important issues of the subjects' life world, such as grades in school, changes in school leadership, and deplorable suburban living conditions. They are not merely 'tape-recording sociologies', in Bourdieu's expression, but the interviewers actively follow up on the subjects' answers, and seek to clarify and extend the interview statements. This concerns obtaining reasons for the teacher's rejection of teamwork, posing critical questions to the pupil believing in a biased grading by his teachers, and challenging the young men's presentations of themselves as innocent victims of harassment. I shall return to the knowledge production in these interview sequences throughout the book.

Interview research in history and in the social sciences

Conversations are an old way of obtaining systematic knowledge. In ancient Greece, Thucydides interviewed participants from the Peloponnesian Wars to write the history of the wars, and Socrates developed philosophical knowledge through dialogues with his Sophist opponents. The term *interview*, is, however, of recent origin; it came into use in the seventeenth century. An interview is literally an *inter-view*, an interchange of views between two persons conversing about a theme of common interest. The first journalistic interview is dated to 1859 with the interview with the Mormon leader Brigham Young published in the *New York Herald Tribune* (Silvester, 1993).

Systematic literature on research interviewing is a new phenomenon of the last few decades. Qualitative interviews have, however, previously been extensively employed in the social sciences. Anthropologists and sociologists have long used informal interviews to obtain knowledge from their informants. Within education and the health sciences, the interview has become a common research method in the last few decades. Turning to my own discipline, I shall give some examples of how qualitative interviews throughout the history of psychology have been a key method for producing scientific and professional knowledge.

- Freud's psychoanalytic theory was to a large extent founded on therapeutic interviews with his patients. His several hundred interviews, an hour long with each patient, were based on the patient's free associations and on the therapist's 'free-hovering attention' (Freud, 1963). These qualitative interviews produced new psychological knowledge about dreams and neuroses, personality and sexuality, knowledge that after a hundred years still has a prominent position in psychological textbooks. Psychoanalysis continues to have a professional impact on psychotherapy, to be of interest to other disciplines and the general public, and to represent a challenge to philosophers.
- Piaget's (1930) theory of child development was based on his interviews with children in natural settings, often in combination with simple experimental tasks. He was trained as a psychoanalyst, and what he termed his 'clinical method' was inspired by the psychoanalytic interview. He let the children talk spontaneously about the weight and size of objects and noticed the manner in which their thoughts unfolded, using a combination of naturalistic observations, simple tests and interviews.
- Experiments on the effects of changes in illumination on production at the Hawthorne Chicago plant of the Western Electrical Company in the 1920s had

led to unexpected results – work output and worker morale improved when the lighting of the production rooms was increased, as well as when it was decreased. These unforeseen findings were followed up in what may have been the largest interview inquiry ever conducted. More than 21,000 workers were each interviewed for over an hour and the interview transcripts analyzed qualitatively and quantitatively. The authors were inspired by therapeutic interviews; they mention the influence of Janet, Freud, Jung, and in particular Piaget, whose clinical method of interviewing children they found particularly useful quantitatively (*Management and the Worker*, Roethlisberger and Dickson, 1939).

- The design and advertisements of consumer products have since the 1950s been extensively investigated by individual qualitative interviews, and in recent decades by interviews in focus groups. One pioneer, Dichter, reports in *The Strategy of Desire* (1960) an interview study he conducted in 1939 on consumer motivation for purchasing a car, with more than a hundred detailed conversational interviews. One main finding was how the importance of a car goes beyond its technical qualities to also encompass its 'personality', which today is commonplace knowledge in marketing. Dichter described his interview technique as inspired by the diagnoses of psychoanalysts and termed it a 'depth interview', and also, inspired by the therapist Carl Rogers, a 'non-directive interview'.

These four historical interview studies have influenced the way we think about men, women and children today, and they have had a major impact on social practices such as therapy, and on techniques for controlling the behaviour of workers and consumers (Kvale, 2003). Freud and Piaget, whose main empirical evidence came from interviews, are still among the psychologists most quoted in scientific literature, and their interpretations of their interviews with patients and children have had a major impact on how we understand personality and childhood today. Thus in *Time Magazine's* (1999) selection of the hundred most influential people of the twentieth century, the only social scientists among the twenty leading 'Scientists and Thinkers' were the economist Keynes and the psychologists Freud and Piaget. The Hawthorne investigations have had a major impact on the organization of industrial production by instigating changes from a 'human engineering' to a 'human relations' mode of managing workers. The marketing of consumer products today rests heavily upon qualitative interviews, in particular in focus groups, to secure maximum prediction and control of the consumers' purchasing behaviour.

In the social sciences today, qualitative interviews are increasingly employed as a research method in their own right, with an expanding methodological literature on how to carry out interview research. Glaser and Strauss's sociological study of hospitals, reported in *The Discovery of Grounded Theory: Strategies for Qualitative Research* (1967), pioneered a qualitative research movement in the social sciences. They used qualitative interviews integrated in their field studies of the hospital world. Two important early books systematically introducing research interviewing were Spradley's *The Ethnographic Interview* (1979) and Mishler's *Research Interviewing – Context and Narrative'* (1986). For an overview of the present scope of research interviewing, the reader is referred to Gubrium and Holstein's *The Handbook of Interview Research* (2002), and for qualitative research more broadly to Denzin and Lincoln's *The Sage Handbook of Qualitative Research* (2005).

Qualitative methods – ranging from participant observation over interviews to discourse analysis – have since the 1980s become key methods of social research. The rapidly growing number of books about qualitative research is one indication of this trend; thus for one leading company – Sage Publications – there was a growth in qualitative books from 10 books in 1980–7 to 130 books in 1995–2002 (Seale et al., 2004). An opening of the social sciences to the humanities has also taken place, drawing on hermeneutics, as well as narrative, discursive, conversational and linguistic forms of analysis (see, e.g., Schwandt, 2001).

Technical, epistemological and cultural reasons may be suggested for the growing use of qualitative research interviews. The availability of small portable tape recorders in the 1950s made the exact recording of interviews easy. In the 1980s, computer programs facilitated the qualitative analyses of transcribed interviews. Broad changes in current thought, reflected in philosophy, emphasize key aspects of interview knowledge. With a linguistic turn in philosophy, conversations, discourses and narratives are regarded as essential for obtaining knowledge of the social world. In addition to this there are phenomenological descriptions of consciousness and of the life world, hermeneutic interpretations of the meaning of texts, and a postmodern emphasis on the social construction of knowledge (see Gibbs, 2007; Rapley, 2007).

Interviews have also become part of the common culture; the current age, as visualized by the talk shows on TV, has been termed an 'interview society' by Atkinson and Silverman (1997), where production of the self has come in focus and the interview serves as a social technique by construction of the self. The authors attribute the prevalence of interviews to the spirit of the age; we may add that in an experiential economy of a consumer society, where the sale of experiences and lifestyles is essential for the economy, qualitative interviews become a key approach in market research to predict and control consumer behaviour.

Methodological and ethical issues

The interview is a conversation that has a structure and a purpose determined by the one party – the interviewer. It is a professional interaction, which goes beyond the spontaneous exchange of views as in everyday conversation, and becomes a careful questioning and listening approach with the purpose of obtaining thoroughly tested knowledge. The qualitative research interview is a construction site for knowledge. One form of research interview – a semi-structured life-world interview – will be in focus throughout this book. It is defined as an interview with the purpose of obtaining descriptions of the life world of the interviewee with respect to interpreting the meaning of the described phenomena.

Within the social sciences the closeness of the research interview to everyday conversations may have implied an illusory simplicity, which has contributed to the popularity of research interviewing – it is too easy to start interviewing without any preceding preparation or reflection. A novice researcher may have a good idea, grab a tape recorder, go out and find some subjects, and start questioning them. The recorded interviews are transcribed and then – during the analysis of the many pages of transcripts – a multitude of problems about the purpose and content of the interviews surface. The likelihood that these spontaneous interview studies lead to worthwhile information is meagre; rather than producing new substantial knowledge about a topic, such interviews may be reproducing common opinions and prejudices. This being said, interviewing can be an exciting way of doing strong and valuable research. The personal interrelationship with the unfolding of stories and new insights can be rewarding for both parties of the interview interaction. Reading the transcribed interviews may inspire the researcher to new interpretations of well-known phenomena. And interviewing can produce substantial new knowledge to a field. Some examples are given throughout this book.

A novice researcher who is methodologically oriented may have a host of questions about technical and conceptual issues in an interview project. For example: How do I begin an interview project? How many subjects will I need? How can I avoid influencing the subjects with leading questions? Can the interviews be of harm to the subjects? Is transcription of the interviews necessary? How do I analyze the interviews? Will my interpretations only be subjective? Can I be sure that I get to know what the subjects really mean? How do I report my extensive interview texts?

If corresponding questions were raised about, for example, a questionnaire survey, several would be fairly easy to answer by consulting authoritative textbooks on standard techniques and rules of survey research. As will appear from the present book, the situation is quite the contrary for the little-standardized craft of qualitative interview research, for which there are few standard rules or common methodological conventions. The reading of this book may then be frustrating, as in lieu of standard procedures and fixed rules, the answers to questions such as those posed above will be in the form 'It depends upon … the specific purpose and topic of an investigation'.

Ethical issues permeate interview research. The knowledge produced depends on the social relationship of interviewer and interviewee, which again rests on the interviewer's ability to create a stage where the subject is free and safe to talk of private events for later public use. This again requires a delicate balance between the interviewer's concern of pursuing interesting knowledge and ethical respect for the integrity of the interview subject. The tension of knowledge and ethics in research interviewing is well expressed in Sennett's book *Respect* (2004, pp. 37–8):

> In-depth interviewing is a distinctive, often frustrating craft. Unlike a pollster asking questions, the in-depth interviewer wants to probe the responses people give. To probe, the interviewer cannot be stonily impersonal; he or she has to give something of himself or herself in order to merit an open response. Yet the conversation lists in one direction; the point is not to talk the way friends do. The interviewer all too frequently finds that he or she has offended subjects, transgressing a line over which only friends or intimates can cross. The craft consists in calibrating social distances without making the subject feel like an insect under the microscope.

▦ Key points

- The qualitative interview is a key venue for exploring the ways in which subjects experience and understand their world. It provides a unique access to the lived world of the subjects, who in their own words describe their activities, experiences and opinions.
- Qualitative interview research has a long history in the social sciences, whereas systematic literature on interview research is a new phenomenon of the last few decades.
- The interview is a powerful method of producing knowledge of the human situation, as demonstrated by historical interview studies, which have changed the ways of understanding the human situation and of managing human behaviour throughout the twentieth century.

Further reading

The following sources will extend this brief introduction to interviewing and qualitative research in more detail:

Denzin, N.K. and Lincoln, Y.S. (eds) (2005) *The Sage Handbook of Qualitative Research* (3rd ed.). Thousand Oaks, CA: Sage.

Fielding, N. (ed.) (2003) *Interviewing*, Vols. I–IV. Thousand Oaks, CA: Sage.

Flick, U. (2006) *An Introduction to Qualitative Research* (3rd ed.). London: Sage.

Gubrium, J.F. and Holstein, J.A. (eds) (2002) *Handbook of Interview Research*. Thousand Oaks, CA: Sage.

Seale, C., Gobo. G., Gubrium, J.F. and Silverman, D. (eds) (2004) *Qualitative Research Practice*. London: Sage.

Silvester, E. (ed.) (1993) *The Penguin Book of Interviews: An Anthology from 1859 to the Present Day*. London: Penguin Books.

2
Epistemological issues of interviewing

Mode of understanding in a qualitative research interview   10
Power asymmetry in qualitative research interviews   14
Research interviews between a philosophical dialogue and a
therapeutic interview   15
The interviewer as a miner or as a traveller   19
Epistemological conceptions of interview knowledge   20

Chapter objectives
After reading this chapter, you should be familiar with

- epistemological conceptions of the kind of knowledge produced when interview conversations are applied for research purposes referring to the philosophy of knowledge;
- the mode of understanding of a qualitative research interview and the power dynamics of the interview situation;
- seeing research interviews in relation to other forms of conversation, such as the philosophical dialogue and a therapeutic conversation;
- the miner and the traveller metaphors of interviewing as a way to contrast different epistemological conceptions of the knowledge produced through interviews; and
- concepts ranging from a positivist conception of interviewing as collecting facts to a postmodern conception of knowledge as socially constructed.

Mode of understanding in a qualitative research interview

A semi-structured life-world interview attempts to understand themes of the lived daily world from the subjects' own perspectives. This interview seeks to obtain descriptions of the interviewees' lived world with respect to interpretation of the meaning of the described phenomena. It comes close to an everyday conversation, but as a professional interview it has a purpose and it involves a specific approach and technique; it is semi-structured – it is neither an open everyday conversation nor a closed questionnaire. I shall now, from a phenomenological perspective, outline twelve aspects of this interview form. It will be outlined in more detail in Chapter 5, whereas other forms of interviewing are addressed in Chapter 6.

Life world

The topic of qualitative research interviews is the interviewee's lived everyday world. The interview is a uniquely sensitive and powerful method for capturing the experiences and lived meanings of the subjects' everyday world. Interviews allow the subjects to convey to others their situation from their own perspective and in their own words. In my interview study, grades were a central theme in the life world of the high school pupils, and the interviews sought to describe and reflect the meaning that grades had to the pupils.

Meaning

The interview seeks to understand the meaning of central themes of the subjects' lived world. The interviewer registers and interprets the meanings of what is said as well as how it is said; he or she should be knowledgeable of the interview topic, be observant of – and able to interpret – vocalization, facial expressions and other bodily gestures. An everyday conversation often takes place on a factual level. A pupil may state: 'I am not as stupid as my grades at the examinations showed, but I have bad study habits.' Common reactions could then concern matters-of-fact: 'What grades did you get?' or 'What are your study habits?' – questions that also may yield important information. A meaning-oriented reply would, in contrast, be something like, 'You feel that the grades are not an adequate measure of your competence?'

A qualitative research interview seeks to cover both a factual and a meaning level, although it is usually more difficult to interview on a meaning level. It is necessary to listen to the explicit descriptions and to the meanings expressed, as well as to what is 'said between the lines'. The interviewer may seek to formulate the implicit message, 'send it back' to the subject, and may obtain an immediate confirmation or disconfirmation of the interpretation of what the interviewee is saying.

Qualitative

The qualitative interview seeks qualitative knowledge as expressed in normal language, it does not aim at quantification. The interview aims at nuanced accounts of different aspects of the interviewee's life world; it works with words and not with numbers. In qualitative interviews, precision in description and stringency in meaning interpretation correspond to exactness in quantitative measurements.

Descriptive

The qualitative interviewer encourages the subjects to describe as precisely as possible what they experience and feel, and how they act. The focus is on nuanced descriptions that depict the qualitative diversity, the many differences and varieties of a phenomenon, rather than on ending up with fixed categorizations.

Specificity

Descriptions of specific situations and actions are elicited, not general opinions. On the basis of comprehensive accounts of specific situations and events, the interviewer will be able to arrive at meanings on a concrete level, instead of general opinions obtained by questions such as 'What is your opinion of grading?' Still, it should be recognized that this type of general opinion question can yield information that is of interest in itself.

Qualified naïveté

The interviewer exhibits openness to new and unexpected phenomena, rather than having ready-made categories and schemes of interpretation. The qualitative interview attempts to obtain descriptions that are as comprehensive and presupposition-less as possible of important themes of the interviewee's life world. Rather than the interviewer posing pre-formulated questions with respect to prepared categories for analysis, the qualified naïveté and a bracketing of presuppositions imply openness to new and unexpected phenomena. The interviewer should be curious, sensitive to what is said – as well as to what is not said – and critical of his or her own presuppositions and hypotheses during the interview. Thus, presuppositionlessness also implies a critical awareness of the interviewer's own presuppositions.

Focus

The interview is focused on particular themes; it is neither strictly structured with standard questions, nor entirely 'non-directive'. Through open questions the interview focuses on the topic of research. It is then up to the subjects to bring forth the dimensions they find important by the theme of inquiry. The interviewer leads the subject towards certain themes, but not to specific opinions about these themes.

Ambiguity

The interviewee's answers are sometimes ambiguous. One statement can imply several possibilities of interpretation, and the subject may also give apparently contradictory statements during an interview. The aim of the qualitative research interview is not to end up with unequivocal and quantifiable meanings on the themes in focus. The task of the interviewer is to clarify, as far as possible, whether the ambiguities and contradictory statements are due to a failure of communication in the interview situation, or whether they reflect genuine inconsistencies, ambivalence and contradictions of an interviewee's life situation. The contradictions of interviewees need not merely be due to faulty communication in the interview, nor to the interviewee's personality, but may be adequate reflections of objective contradictions in the world in which they live.

Change

In the course of an interview, subjects can change their descriptions of, and meanings about, a theme. The subjects may themselves discover new aspects of the themes they are describing, and suddenly see relations that they have not been aware of earlier. The questioning can thus instigate processes of reflection where the meanings of themes described by the subjects are no longer the same after the interview. An interview may be a learning process for the interviewee, as well as for the interviewer.

Sensitivity

Different interviewers, using the same interview guide, may produce different statements on the same themes, due to varying levels of sensitivity towards, and knowledge about, the topic of the interview. Thus an interviewer who has no ear for music may have difficulties obtaining nuanced descriptions of musical experiences from his or her interviewees, in particular if trying to probe more intensively into the meaning of the music. If a common methodological requirement of obtaining intersubjectively reproducible data were to be followed here, the interview form might have to be standardized in a way that would restrict the understanding of musical experiences to more superficial aspects understandable to the average interviewee. The requirement of sensitivity to, and a foreknowledge about, the topic of the interview contrasts with the presuppositionless attitude advocated above. The tension between these two aspects may be expressed in the requirement for a qualified naïveté on the part of the interviewer.

Interpersonal situation

The research interview is an inter-view where knowledge is constructed in the inter-action between two people. The interviewer and the subject act in relation to each other and reciprocally influence each other. The knowledge produced in a research interview is constituted by the interaction itself, in the specific situation created between an interviewer and an interviewee. With another interviewer, a different interaction may be created and a different knowledge produced.

Positive experience

A well-conducted research interview may be a rare and enriching experience for the subject, who may obtain new insights into his or her life situation. The interaction may also be anxiety-provoking and evoke defence mechanisms in the interviewee as well as in the interviewer. The interviewer should be aware of and able to address the interpersonal dynamics within an interview. It is probably not a very common experience in everyday life that another person – for an hour or more – shows an interest in, is sensitive towards, and seeks to understand as well as possible one's own experiences and views on a topic. In practice, it may sometimes be difficult to terminate a qualitative interview, as the subjects may want to continue the conversation and explore further the insights in their life world brought about by the interview.

Power asymmetry in qualitative research interviews

Taking account of the mutual understanding and of the personal interview interaction described above, we should not regard a research interview as an open dialogue between egalitarian partners. The research interview is a specific professional conversation with a clear power asymmetry between the researcher and the subject. The asymmetry of the power relation in the research interviewer outlined in Box 2.1 is easily overlooked if we focus only on the open mode of understanding and the close personal interaction of the interview. There does not need to be any intentional exertion of power by the interviewer; the description concerns the structural positions in the interview, whereby for example subjects may, more or less deliberately, tell what they believe the interviewer authority wants to hear.

Box 2.1 Power asymmetry in qualitative research interviews

The interview entails an asymmetrical power relation. The research interview is not an open everyday conversation between equal partners. The interviewer

(Continued)

(Continued)

has a scientific competence, he or she initiates and defines the interview situation, determines the interview topic, poses questions and decides which answers to follow up, and also terminates the conversation.

The interview is a one-way dialogue. An interview is a one-directional questioning – the role of the interviewer is to ask and the role of the interviewee is to answer.

The interview is an instrumental dialogue. In the research interview an instrumentalization of the conversation takes place. A good conversation is no longer a goal in itself, but a means for providing the researcher with descriptions, narratives and texts, to interpret and report according to his or her research interests.

The interview may be a manipulative dialogue. A research interview may follow a more or less hidden agenda. The interviewer may want to obtain information without the interviewee knowing what the interviewer is after, attempting to 'by indirections find directions out'.

The interviewer has a monopoly of interpretation. The researcher usually upholds a monopoly of interpretation over the subject's statements. As the 'big interpreter', the researcher maintains an exclusive privilege to interpret and report what the interviewee really meant.

Counter-control. In reaction to the dominance of the interviewer, some subjects will withhold information, or talk around the subject, and some may start to question the researcher and also protest at his or her questions and interpretations, or, in rare cases, withdraw from the interview.

Exceptions. Some interviewers attempt to reduce the power asymmetry of the interview situation by collaborative interviewing where the researcher and subject approach equality in questioning, interpreting and reporting.

Research interviews between a philosophical dialogue and a therapeutic interview

In the spontaneous conversations of daily life attention will tend to be on the conversation topic, whereas the purpose and the structure of the conversation is seldom addressed. In contrast, professional interviews, such as a therapeutic interview, a job interview or a legal interrogation, are characterized by a focus on the dynamics of interaction between interviewer and interviewee, a methodological awareness of question forms, and a critical attention to what is said. In order to highlight the specific interaction of the research interview I shall compare it to two other forms of conversation – a philosophical dialogue and a therapeutic interview.

Box 2.2   A philosophical dialogue on love

And quite properly, my friend, said Socrates; 'then, such being the case, must not Love be only love of beauty, and not of ugliness?' He assented.

'Well then, we have agreed that he loves what he lacks and has not?'

'Yes,' he replied.

'And what Love lacks and has not is beauty?'

'That needs must be,' he said.

'Well now, will you say that what lacks beauty, and in no wise possesses it, is beautiful?'

'Surely not.'

'So can you still allow Love to be beautiful, if this is the case?'

Whereupon Agathon said, 'I greatly fear, Socrates, I know nothing of what I was talking about.'

Source: Plato (1953, p. 167).

Plato's *Symposion* is a *philosophical dialogue* in a dramatic form. The partners of the dialogue are formally on an equal level, there is a reciprocal questioning of the true nature of the knowledge under debate, as well as of the logic of the participants' questions and answers. In the passage presented in Box 2.2, Socrates takes Agathon's speech on love as his point of departure. He repeats the main points in a condensed form, interprets what Agathon has said, and then asks for his opponent's confirmations or disconfirmations of the interpretations. Socrates had started out by appearing naïve and innocent, and praised Agathon's views on Eros, after which he follows up, such as in the above sequence, by uncovering one contradiction after another in Agathon's position. This philosophical dialogue is a harsh form of interaction that seeks true knowledge through the unrelenting rigour of a discursive argumentation. Socrates compared himself to a legal interrogator and his opponents likened him to an electric eel.

Research interviews today tend to be less agonistic; the interview subject is commonly regarded as an informant or a partner, not as an opponent. The interviewer poses questions in order to obtain knowledge about the interviewee's world, and rarely enters into tenacious arguments about the logic and truth of what the interviewee says. Moreover, it is outside the scope of research interviews for the interviewer to argue the strength of his or her own conception of the topic investigated, or to try to change the subject's convictions.

In contrast, a *therapeutic interview* aims at change through an emotional personal interaction rather than through logical argumentation. The changes sought are not primarily conceptual, but emotional and personal. Although the main purpose of therapeutic interviews is to assist patients to overcome their suffering, a side-effect has been the production of knowledge about the human situation. Both a therapeutic and a research interview may lead to increased understanding and change, but with the emphasis on knowledge production in a research interview and on personal change in a therapeutic interview.

Box 2.3 A therapeutic interview on hate

Subject: *(Silent for two minutes. Does not look at counsellor.)* You feel I want to come, but I *don't!* I'm not coming any more. It doesn't do any good. I don't like you. I hate you! I wish you never were born.

Counsellor: You just hate me very bitterly.

Subject: I think I'll throw you in the lake. I'll cut you up! You think people like you, but they don't. ... You think you can attract women, but you *can't.* ... I wish you were *dead.*

Counsellor: You *detest* me and you'd really like to get rid of me.

Subject: You think my father did bad things with me, but he didn't! You think he wasn't a good man, but he *was.* You think I want intercourse, but I *don't.*

Counsellor: You feel I *absolutely misrepresent* all your thoughts.

...

Subject: You think I haven't been straight, but I have. I *hate* you. All I've had is pain, pain, pain. You think I can't direct my own life, but I can. You think I can't get well, but I can. You think I had hallucinations, but I didn't. I hate you. *(Long pause. Leans on desk in strained, exhausted pose.)* You think I'm crazy, but I'm not.

Counsellor: You're sure I think you're crazy.

Subject: *(Pause.)* I'm tied, and I just can't get loose! *(Despairing tone of voice, and tears. Pause.)* I had a hallucination and I've *got* to get it out!

...

Subject: I knew at the office I had to get rid of this somewhere. I felt I could come down and tell you. I knew you'd understand. I couldn't say I hated myself. That's true but I couldn't say it. So I just thought of all the ugly things I could say to you instead.

Counsellor: The things you felt about yourself you couldn't say, but you could say them about me.

Subject: I know we're getting to rock bottom. ...

Source: Rogers (1956, pp. 211–13).

Carl Rogers was a therapist who pioneered in developing an open, client-centred interview form, originally termed *non-directive* and later changed to *client-centred*, with the insight that all interviewing implies a sense of direction. Rogers was critical towards Freud's theories of the unconscious and the speculative interpretations of psychoanalysis. Although their theoretical conceptions differed strongly, the client-centred interview in Box 2.3 comes fairly close to psychoanalytic interview practice. This concerns the intense emotional interaction as well as the few and cautious responses of the therapist. The interview was conducted by a counsellor applying Rogers's therapeutic interview technique, an approach that was an inspiration for the early use of qualitative research interviews.

In this session the client takes the lead right from the start, introduces the theme important to her – the detestable counsellor – and tells how much she hates him. He responds by reflecting and rephrasing her statements, emphasizing their emotional aspects. He does not, as would be likely in a normal conversation, take issue with the many accusations against him. In this sequence the counsellor neither asks questions for clarification, nor does he offer interpretations. At the end, after 'she has got it all out', the client acknowledges the counsellor's ability to understand her, and she herself offers an interpretation: I couldn't say I hated myself, so I just thought of all the ugly things I could say to you instead. We may note that the counsellor's interventions were not entirely non-directive; the client introduces several themes – such as not wanting to come to therapy, it does not do her any good, and objecting to the therapist's belief that her father did wrong things with her – whereas the counsellor consistently repeats and condenses her negative statements about himself, which leads the client to an emotional insight.

This therapeutic sequence indicates the possibilities for research interviewers to learn from the techniques developed within the therapeutic profession, while also demonstrating differences between therapeutic and research interviews. While the interviewer's repetitions and rephrasing of the subject's statements are characteristic of many research interviews, the personal conflicts and strong emotional reactions provoked in the therapeutic session are ethically beyond the bounds of research interviewing. The long intensive personal therapeutic relationship may trigger painful, hidden memories and give access to deeper levels of personality, which are hardly accessible, and ethically off limits, in a short research interview. The purpose of a research interview is to produce knowledge about the phenomena investigated, and any changes in the interviewed subject are a side-effect. The aim of a therapeutic interview is the facilitation of changes in the patient, and the general knowledge of the human situation gained in the therapeutic process is a side-effect of helping patients to overcome their neurotic suffering.

Taking account of such important differences, it is still possible for research interviewers today to learn from therapeutic interviews. This concerns establishing contact – 'rapport', the modes of questioning and listening, and the interpretation of meaning developed in therapeutic interviews. Just as important as learning from therapeutic interviews, the research interviewer needs to discern methodically and ethically therapeutic and research interviewing. Freud thus warned against scientifically formulating a case during treatment, because that would interfere with the open therapeutic attitude with which one proceeds 'aimlessly, and allows oneself to be overtaken by any surprises, always presenting to them an open mind, free from any expectations' (1963, p. 120). And when personal expressions and emotions are encouraged in a research interview, the researcher should take care that it does not turn into a therapeutic situation, which falls outside an explicit or implicit interview contract, and which the researcher may not be qualified to handle.

The interviewer as a miner or as a traveller

I shall now turn from the mode of understanding of the research interview and its relation to other forms of interviews, to conceptions of the knowledge produced in the interview interaction. Two contrasting metaphors of the interviewer – as a miner or as a traveller – may illustrate the different epistemological conceptions of interviewing as a process of knowledge collection or as a process of knowledge construction, respectively. By metaphor I refer to understanding one thing by means of another thing. The two metaphors for interviewing, although not logically distinct categories, may inspire the researcher to reflect upon what conceptions of knowledge he or she brings to an interview inquiry.

In a *miner metaphor*, knowledge is understood as buried metal and the interviewer is a miner who unearths the valuable metal. The knowledge is waiting in the subject's interior to be uncovered, uncontaminated by the miner. The interviewer digs nuggets of knowledge out of a subject's pure experiences, unpolluted by any leading questions. The nuggets may be conceived as objective real data or as subjective authentic meanings. A research interviewer strips the surface of conscious experience, whereas a therapeutic interviewer mines the deeper unconscious layers. By means of a variety of data-mining procedures the researcher extracts the objective facts or the essential meanings, today preferably by computer programs. We should note that the miner metaphor does not only pertain to a positivist and empiricist data collection, but also to Socrates' pursuits for truths already existing and to Freud's quest for hidden meanings buried in the unconscious.

An alternative *traveller metaphor* understands the interviewer as a traveller on a journey to a distant country that leads to a tale to be told upon returning home. The interviewer-traveller wanders through the landscape and enters into conversations with the people he or she encounters. The traveller explores the many domains of the country, as unknown territory or with maps, roaming freely around the territory. The interview traveller, in line with the original Latin meaning of conversation as 'wandering together with', walks along with the local inhabitants, asks questions and encourages them to tell their own stories of their lived world. The potentialities of meanings in the original stories are differentiated and unfolded through the traveller's interpretations in the narratives he or she brings back to home audiences. The journey may not only lead to new knowledge; the traveller might change as well. The journey might instigate a process of reflection that leads the traveller to new ways of self-understanding, as well as uncovering previously taken-for-granted values and customs in the traveller's home country.

The two metaphors – of the interviewer as a miner or as a traveller – represent different concepts of knowledge production. Each metaphor stands for alternative genres and has different rules of the game. A miner approach will tend to regard interviews as a site of data collection separated from the later data analysis. A traveller conception leads to interviewing and analysis as intertwined phases of knowledge construction, with an emphasis on the narrative to be told to an audience. The data-mining conception of interviewing is close to the mainstream of modern social sciences where knowledge is already there, waiting to be found, whereas the traveller conception is nearer to anthropology and a postmodern comprehension of knowledge as socially constructed.

Epistemological conceptions of interview knowledge

The interview is a special form of conversational practice, which has developed in everyday life over centuries, and which was institutionalized as journalistic interviews in the middle of the nineteenth century and as therapeutic interviews in the early twentieth century. Research interviews have not been developed from any specific theory or epistemological paradigm. We may, however, post hoc invoke theoretical and epistemological positions to understand the knowledge produced in interviews. A clarification of such positions may serve to shed light on different conceptions and practices of research interviewing.

I shall now mention philosophically reflected conceptions of knowledge with different implications for research interviewing. First I briefly describe hermeneutics and phenomenology and then go on to the contrasting positions of a positivist versus a postmodern epistemology on interview knowledge, which imply a miner and a traveller metaphor of interviewing, respectively (see Kvale, 1996a, and Schwandt, 2001, for more extensive presentations of these epistemologies in relation to qualitative research).

Key terms used in describing the mode of understanding of the interview above – such as experience, consciousness, meaning, interpretation and human interrelations – are taken from the vernacular. Within phenomenological and hermeneutical philosophy, these terms have been the subject of systematic reflection. The *phenomenological* philosophy of Husserl and Merleau-Ponty thus describes and analyzes consciousness, it focuses on the life world, with openness to the experiences of the subjects; there is a primacy of precise descriptions, attempts to bracket foreknowledge, and a search for invariant essential meanings in the descriptions. In the *hermeneutical* tradition of the humanities, taken up in the last century by Gadamer and Ricouer, the interpretation of the meaning of texts is the central endeavour. The concepts of conversation and text are essential, there is an emphasis on the multiplicity of meanings in a text, and on the interpreter's foreknowledge of a text's subject matter.

A *positivist* epistemology has dominated earlier social science textbooks on methodology; truth was to be found through method, by following general rules of method that were largely independent of the content and context of the investigation. Scientific statements should be based upon observable data; the observation of the data and the interpretation of their meanings were to be strictly separated. The scientific facts were to be unambiguous, intra-subjectively and inter-subjectively reproducible, objective and quantifiable. Scientific statements ought to be value-neutral, facts were to be distinguished from values, and science from ethics and politics. Any influence by the person of the researcher should be eliminated or minimized.

To a philosophy of science that takes as its point of departure the elimination of the human factor in research, key aspects of the mode of understanding in qualitative research interviews appear as methodological sources of error. A strict positivist philosophy is hardly compatible with knowledge production in qualitative interviews, and it is seldom explicitly advocated today. However, we should not overlook the historical contribution of Comte's positivist philosophy in bringing social science from metaphysical speculation to empirical observations, and the subsequent emphasis upon transparency and control of research procedures in order to counteract subjective and ideological bias in research.

In a *postmodern* approach the qualitative research interview appears as a construction site of knowledge. The knowledge generated by interviews is in line with key features of a postmodern conception of knowledge, such as the conversational, the narrative, the linguistic, the contextual and interrelational nature of knowledge. With a decline of modern universal systems of knowledge, the local, manifold and changing language contexts come into prominence (Lyotard, 1984). With the heterogeneity of contexts, the issues of translations come into the foreground, such as from oral interviews to written texts, and from private interview conversations to public conversations. In a postmodern epistemology the certainty of our knowledge is less a matter of interaction with a non-human reality than a matter of conversation between persons. Knowledge is interrelational, interwoven in webs of networks. With a breakdown of global meta-narratives of legitimation, there is an emphasis on the local context, on the social and linguistic construction of a perspectival reality where knowledge is validated through practice. The qualitative research interview is a construction site of knowledge. An interview is literally an inter-view, an inter-change of views between two persons conversing about a common theme. Here knowledge is constituted through linguistic interaction, where the participants' discourse, its structures and effects, is of interest in its own right. The interview gives access to the manifold of local narratives embodied in storytelling and opens for a discourse and negotiation of the meaning of the lived world.

In the pragmatic approach of the present book, the emphasis is less on paradigmatic legitimation of interview research than on the practical implications of the different epistemological positions for interview research. In later chapters I will give examples of how different epistemological positions lead to different conceptions of interview research, and also to different practice, by the many how-to-do decisions throughout an interview investigation. This concerns the understanding and use of leading questions (Chapter 7), interview analysis (Chapter 9), reliability and objectivity of interview knowledge (Chapter 10) and reporting an interview inquiry (Chapter 11). In the following Chapter 3 on ethics I shall discuss how, with a dissolution of the dichotomy of facts and values and a loss of faith in knowledge as objective and progressive, the ethical dimensions of knowledge production become pivotal, not only as ethical guidelines for research, but as social research itself becomes a moral endeavour.

▨ Key points

- Key terms of the mode of understanding of a semi-structured life-world interview involve: life world, meaning, qualitative, descriptive, specificity, qualified naïveté, focused, ambiguity, change, sensitivity, interaction and a positive experience.
- A professional research interview is not an egalitarian dialogue among equal partners, but entails a specific power asymmetry where the interviewer sets the stage for the interview, controls the sequence, and uses the outcome for his or her purposes.
- The qualitative research interview has affinities to philosophical dialogues as well as to therapeutic interviews, but follows neither the relentless intellectual reasoning of the former nor the close personal interaction of the latter.
- The two metaphors of the interviewer as a miner and as a traveller, involve contrasting conceptions of the interviewer, as respectively a knowledge collector or a knowledge producer.
- The epistemological understanding of the interview varies from positivist conceptions of interviewing as a collection of facts to a postmodern conception of interviewing as a social construction of knowledge.

Further reading

The background of doing interviews is further unfolded in these three sources:

Kvale, S. (1996a) *InterViews – An Introduction to Qualitative Research Interviewing*. Thousand Oaks, CA: Sage.
Rosenau, M.P. (1992) *Postmodernism and the Social Sciences*. Princeton, NJ: Princeton University Press.
Schwandt, T.A. (2001) *Dictionary of Qualitative Inquiry*. Thousand Oaks, CA: Sage.

3
Ethical issues of interviewing

Interviewing as a moral inquiry   23
Ethical issues throughout an interview inquiry   24
Ethical guidelines   25
Micro- and macro-ethics in interview studies   30

Chapter objectives
After reading this chapter, you should understand

- how interviewing for research purposes involves moral concerns;
- how ethical issues go beyond the live interview situation and are embedded in all stages of an interview inquiry;
- ethical guidelines for social research and the importance of informed consent, confidentiality, consequences and the researcher role; and
- how moral issues of interviewing go beyond the micro-ethics of an interview project to include the macro-ethics of the broader social effects of the interview-produced knowledge.

Interviewing as a moral inquiry

An interview inquiry is a moral enterprise. Moral issues concern the means as well as the ends of an interview inquiry. The human interaction in the interview affects the interviewees and the knowledge produced by an interview inquiry affects our understanding of the human condition. Consequently, interview research is saturated with moral and ethical issues. Ethical problems in interview research arise particularly because of the complexities of 'researching private lives and placing accounts in the public arena' (Mauthner et al., 2002, p. 1).

The undertaking of a research project raises questions as to the value of the knowledge produced, what will be the social contributions of the study. Social science research should serve scientific *and* human interests. The preamble to the

American Psychological Association's ethical principles thus emphasized that psychologists are committed to increasing knowledge of human behaviour and of people's understanding of themselves and others, and to utilizing this knowledge for the promotion of human welfare, thus:'The decision to undertake research rests upon a considered judgment by the individual psychologist about how best to contribute to psychological science and human welfare' (APA, 1981, p. 637).

Box 3.1 Ethical issues at seven research stages

Thematizing. The purpose of an interview study should, beyond the scientific value of the knowledge sought, also be considered with regard to improvement of the human situation investigated.

Designing. Ethical issues of design involve obtaining the subjects' informed consent to participate in the study, securing confidentiality, and considering the possible consequences of the study for the subjects.

Interview situation. The consequences of the interview interaction for the subjects need to be taken into account, such as stress during the interview and changes in self-understanding.

Transcription. The confidentiality of the interviewees needs to be protected and there is also the question of whether a transcribed text is loyal to the interviewee's oral statements.

Analysis. Ethical issues in analysis involve the question of how penetratingly the interviews can be analyzed and of whether the subjects should have a say in how their statements are interpreted.

Verification. It is the researcher's ethical responsibility to report knowledge that is as secured and verified as possible. This involves the issue of how critically an interviewee may be questioned.

Reporting. There is again the issue of confidentiality when reporting private interviews in public, and of consequences of the published report for the interviewees and for the groups they belong to.

Ethical issues throughout an interview inquiry

Ethical issues go through the entire process of an interview investigation, and potential ethical concerns should be taken into consideration from the very start of an investigation and up to the final report. Some of the ethical concerns that can arise throughout the seven stages of an interview inquiry are depicted in Box 3.1. These stages will be treated in more detail in the following Chapter 4 on designing an investigation. Ethical issues such as those presented above need be considered when preparing an *ethical protocol* for an interview study. Within some fields, such as in the health sciences, it is mandatory to submit an interview project to an ethical review board before the investigation may be undertaken. The researcher is thereby required to think through in advance value issues and ethical dilemmas that may arise during an interview project, and perhaps also be encouraged to consult experienced members in the research community.

Even when not a formal requirement, it may be of value when planning an interview inquiry to also draft a parallel ethical protocol treating ethical issues that can be anticipated in an investigation. With a foreknowledge of the moral issues that typically arise at the different stages of an interview investigation, the researcher can make reflected choices while designing a study and be alert to critical and sensitive issues that may turn up during the inquiry.

The difficulty of specifying in advance the topics of interview studies, which are often exploratory, as well as of describing in advance the specific questions to be posed in a flexible non-standardized interview, constitutes, however, a potential problem with some ethical review boards. Some boards may want to approve every interview question in advance, which may be feasible for the pre-determined questions in a questionnaire, whereas open research interviews involve on-the-spot decisions about following up unanticipated leads from the subjects with questions that cannot be determined in advance.

Parker (2005) has criticized ethics committees in the United Kingdom for favouring quantitative over qualitative approaches, indirectly preventing new forms of research that have not been described in the code, and for being bureaucratic in their use of checklists, often with the result that researchers spend their time trying to get through the review process instead of engaging in serious thought about ethics. In the United States, the institutional review boards (IRBs) and their ethical guidelines for human subjects research have likewise been criticized for serving a new methodological conservatism constraining participatory qualitative research (Lincoln, 2005). Developed for experimentation in biomedical research, these guidelines have been extrapolated to the social sciences, where to a large extent they are incongruent with interpretative and interactive qualitative research methods such as interviewing, field research and participatory action research. While fully informed consent is highly pertinent in high-risk medical experiments, it is less relevant and feasible in low-risk field studies and interviews. Lincoln further argues that with the reconfigured relationships of qualitative research as cooperative, mutual, democratic and open-ended, key issues of common ethical guidelines become non-issues in a feminist communitarian ethics.

Ethical guidelines

Professional ethical codes serve as contexts for reflection on the specific ethical decisions throughout an interview inquiry. Philosophical ethical theories provide frames for more extended ethical reflection; key positions are here a Kantian ethics of duty, a utilitarian ethics of consequences and Aristotle's virtue ethics (Kimmel, 1988), and, more recently a caring communitarian ethics (Lincoln 2005). Such conceptual contexts seldom provide definite answers to the normative choices to be made during a research project; they are more like texts to be interpreted with respect to their relevance to specific situations. Examples and case studies may serve as aids for the transition from general principles to specific practices. The ethical skills embodied in local professional communities further represent an important extension of the written ethical principles, rules and examples.

Box 3.2   Ethical questions at the start of an interview study

What are the *beneficial* consequences of the study?

How can the study contribute to enhancing the situation of the participating subject? Of the group they represent? Of the human condition?

How can the *informed consent* of the participating subjects be obtained?

How much information about the study needs to be given in advance, and what can wait until a debriefing after the interviews?

Who should give the consent – the subjects or their superiors?

How can the *confidentiality* of the interview subjects be protected?

How important is it that the subjects remain anonymous?

How can the identity of the subjects be disguised?

Who will have access to the interviews?

Can legal problems concerning protection of the subjects' anonymity be expected?

What are the *consequences* of the study for the participating subjects?

Will any potential harm to the subjects be outweighed by potential benefits?

Will the interviews approximate therapeutic relationships, and if so, what precautions can be taken?

When publishing the study, what consequences may be anticipated for the subjects and for the groups they represent?

How will the *researcher's role* affect the study?

How can a researcher avoid co-option from the funding of a project or over-identification with his or her subjects, thereby losing critical perspective on the knowledge produced?

Ethical guidelines for social science research commonly concern the subjects' informed consent to participate in the study, confidentiality of the subjects, consequences of participation in the research project and the researcher's role in the study (cf. *Guidelines for the Protection of Human Subjects*, 1992). Box 3.2 outlines issues raised by these ethical guidelines in the form of questions, which interviewers may ask themselves before embarking on an interview journey.

Informed consent

Informed consent entails informing the research subjects about the overall purpose of the investigation and the main features of the design, as well as of possible risks and benefits from participation in the research project. This raises the issue of how informed consent can be handled in exploratory interview studies where the investigators themselves will have little advance knowledge of how the interviews will proceed. Informed consent further involves obtaining the voluntary participation of subjects and informing them about their right to withdraw from the study at any time.

Through briefing and debriefing, the interviewees should be informed about the purpose and the procedure of the interview. This may include information about confidentiality and who will have access to the interview; the researcher's right to publish the whole interview or parts of it; and the interviewee's possible access to the transcription and the analyses of the interviews. In most cases such issues may not matter much to the subjects. If, however, it is likely that the investigation may treat or instigate issues of conflict, particularly within institutional settings, a written agreement may serve as a protection for both the interviewees and the researcher. In particular, when it comes to later use of the interview it may be preferable to have a written agreement on the informed consent of the interviewee to participate in the study and the future use of the interviews, signed by both interviewer and subject (see Yow, 1994, for examples of letters of agreement with subjects).

Issues about *who should give the consent* may arise with interviews in institutions, where a superior's consent to a study may imply a more or less subtle pressure on employees to participate. With school children, the question comes up about who should give the consent – the children themselves, their parents, the teacher, the school superintendent or the school board?

Informed consent also involves the question of *how much information should be given and when*. Full information about design and purpose counteracts deception of the subjects. Providing information about a study involves a careful balance between detailed over-information and leaving out aspects of the design that may be significant to the subjects. In some interview investigations, such as those using funnel-shaped techniques (Chapter 5), the specific purposes of a study are initially withheld in order to obtain the interviewees' spontaneous views on a topic and to avoid leading them to specific answers. In such cases full information should be given in a debriefing after the interview.

Confidentiality

Confidentiality in research implies that private data identifying the subjects will not be reported. If a study does publish information potentially recognizable to others, the subjects need to agree on the release of identifiable information. The principle of the research subjects' right to privacy is not without ethical and scientific dilemmas. Thus there is a concern about what information should be available to whom. Should, for example, interviews with children be available to their parents and teachers? In studies where several parties are involved, such as by individual interviews within organizations, or with married or divorced couples, it should be made clear before the interviewing who will later have access to the interviews. In extreme cases, protecting confidentiality can raise serious legal problems, for example if a researcher – through the promise of confidentiality and the trust of the relationship – has obtained knowledge of mistreatment, malpractice, child abuse, the use of drugs or other criminal behaviour either on the part of the interviewee or others.

The qualitative research interview involves different ethical issues from those of a questionnaire survey, where confidentiality is assured by the computed averages of survey responses. In a qualitative study where subjects' statements from a private interview setting may be published in public reports, precautions need to be taken to protect the subjects' privacy. Here there may be an intrinsic conflict between ethical demands for confidentiality and basic principles of scientific research, such as providing the necessary information for inter-subjective control and for repeating a study. We should also note that in some cases interviewees, who have spent their time and provided valuable information to the researcher, may want, as is usual in journalistic interviews, to be credited with their full name. Parker (2005) has argued that anonymity of the subjects may actually serve to protect the researcher, denying the subjects a voice in the research project. The subjects' anonymity may serve as an alibi for the researcher in retaining the privilege of controlling and disseminating the information about the study. Parker thus advocates discussing openly with those who take part in research whether or not they might actually prefer to be named and to speak openly for themselves.

Consequences

The consequences of an interview study need to be addressed with respect to possible harm to the subjects as well as to the expected benefits of participating in the study. The ethical principle of *beneficence* means that the risk of harm to a subject should be the least possible. From a utilitarian ethical perspective, the sum of potential benefits to a subject and the importance of the knowledge gained should outweigh the risk of harm to the subject and thus warrant a decision to carry out the study (*Guidelines*, 1992, p. 15). This involves a researcher's responsibility to reflect on the possible consequences not only for the persons taking part in the study, but for the larger group they belong to as well.

An interviewer should take into account that the openness and intimacy of the interview may be seductive and can lead subjects to disclose information they may later regret. A research interviewer's ability to listen attentively may also in some cases lead to quasi-therapeutic relationships, for which most research interviewers are not trained; compare here the challenges to the therapeutic interviewer reported in Box 2.3. In particular, long and repeated interviews on personal topics may lead to quasi-therapeutic relations. The personal closeness of the interview relation puts strong demands on the ethical sensitivity and respect of the interviewer regarding how far to go in his or her questioning.

The integrity of the researcher

The researcher as a person is critical for the quality of the scientific knowledge and for the soundness of ethical decisions in an interview inquiry. Moral research behaviour involves more than ethical knowledge and cognitive choices; it encompasses the moral integrity of the researcher, his or her sensitivity and commitment to moral issues and action. By interviewing, the importance of the researcher as a person is magnified because the interviewer is the main instrument for obtaining knowledge. Being familiar with value issues, ethical guidelines and ethical theories may help in choices that weigh ethical versus scientific concerns in a study. In the end, however, the integrity of the researcher – his or her knowledge, experience, honesty and fairness – is the decisive factor. With the dependence on the ethical judgements of the researcher, it becomes important to foster the ethical skills of interview researchers. These may be promoted by the study of ethically complex cases of interview research, and by conversations with peers and representatives of the subjects studied (Brinkmann and Kvale, 2005).

The independence of research can be co-opted from 'above' as well as from 'below' by those funding a project, as well as by its participants. Ties to either group may lead the researcher to ignore some findings and emphasize others to the detriment of an investigation of the phenomena being as comprehensive and unbiased as possible. Interviewing is interactive research; through close interpersonal interactions with their subjects, interviewers may be particularly prone to attempts at coalition making by them. Interviewers may identify with their subjects so closely that they do not maintain a professional distance, but instead report and interpret everything from their subjects' perspectives – in anthropological terms, 'going native'.

The role of the interviewer can involve a tension between a professional distance and a personal friendship. Thus in the context of a feminist, caring, committed ethic, the interviewer has been conceived as a friend, as a warm and caring researcher. This early conception of the interviewer as a caring friend has later been criticized from a feminist standpoint. Duncombe and Jessop (2002) argue that an interviewer's show of intimacy and empathy may involve a faking of friendship and commodification of rapport, sanitized of any concern with broader ethical issues. When under pressure to deliver results, whether to a commercial employer or to their own thesis, the interviewer's show of empathy may become a means to circumvent the subject's informed consent and persuade interviewees to disclose experiences and emotions that they later on might have preferred to keep to themselves or even 'not know'. In the expression of a therapist researcher, Fog (2004), an experienced interviewer's knowledge of how to create rapport and to get through a subject's defences may serve as a 'Trojan horse' to get inside areas of a person's life where they were not invited. The use of such indirect techniques, which are ethically legitimate within the joint interest of a therapeutic relationship, becomes ethically questionable when applied to research and commercial purposes.

Micro- and macro-ethics in interview studies

Ethical issues in interview research tend to be raised in relation to the personal implications for the subjects, whereas the wider social consequences of the interviews have received less attention. In line with the common treatments of research ethics, I have focused above on the *micro-ethics* of the interview situation and of possible future consequences for the subjects involved. I shall now go on to draw in a *macro-ethical perspective* and address potential consequences of the knowledge produced by interviews in a broader social situation (cf. Brinkmann and Kvale, 2005). By drawing upon the historical interview investigations presented in Chapter 1, I shall point out potential conflicts between ethical demands from a micro- and a macro-perspective.

Ethical issues may differ when viewed from a micro- and a macro-perspective. An interview situation may be experienced positively by the subject, when a researcher with a professional authority shows a strong interest in what he or she has to say. The wider social consequences of the knowledge produced in such interviews may, however, be problematic in some cases. This concerns the Hawthorne studies by the management of how to manage the workers more efficiently and increase their output, and today in particular when interviewing for increased consumption. Consumer interviews as individual motivational interviews or as focus groups may well follow standard ethical guidelines and also be enjoyable to the participants. On a macro-level, however, the consequences are more questionable. Focus group interviews about teenager attitudes to smoking may provide knowledge for improving advertisements to teenagers for smoking, or the knowledge produced may be used in health campaigns to discourage smoking. In a capitalist consumer society it is likely that there will be more capital available for producing and applying knowledge on smoking attitudes for the tobacco industry's advertisements to increase tobacco consumption than for public campaigns seeking to reduce the use of tobacco.

Tensions of ethics on a micro- and a macro-level also arise in academic interview research. We may here draw in a historic study on anti-Semitism – *The Authoritarian Personality* by Adorno et al. (1950). In the wake of the Second World War the researchers investigated a possible relation of anti-Semitism to an authoritarian upbringing. An important part of the study consisted of therapeutically inspired interviews, where the researchers used therapeutic techniques to circumvent their subjects' defences in order to learn about their prejudices and authoritarian personality traits. On a micro-level this research clearly violated the ethical principle of informed consent, whereas on a macro-level the knowledge obtained of the roots of anti-Semitism was intended to have beneficial social and political consequences.

Ethical issues on a macro-level can ideally be approached by public discussion of the social consequences and uses of the knowledge produced. We may here draw in an interview study by Bellah and co-workers (1985) about individualism and commitment in America, to be discussed in Chapter 6. The researchers saw the very aim of doing social science as a public philosophy, as engaging in debate with the public about the goals and values of society:'When data from such interviews are well presented, they stimulate the reader to enter the conversation, to argue with what is being said. Curiously, such interviews stimulate something that could be called public opinion, opinion tested in the arena of open discussion' (Bellah et al., 1985, p. 305).

▤ Key points

- With the production of interview knowledge through the interaction of the interviewer and interviewee, close attention needs to be given to the ethical implications of this personal interaction.
- Ethical issues raised by an interview study go beyond the live interview situation itself, to encompass all stages of an interview project.
- Ethical guidelines for social science research emphasize the need to obtain the subjects' informed consent to participate in the study, to secure the confidentiality of the subjects, to consider the consequences for the subjects of participation in the research project and to be attentive to the researcher's role in the study.
- Ethical requirements for research are mostly formulated in a general form. With few standard rules to be followed, much is left to the judgement of the researcher. Thus an interviewer continually has to make on-the-spot decisions about what implications of an answer to follow up, and what connotations may be too sensitive for the interviewee to be followed up.
- With the person of the interviewer being the instrument of interview research, ethical decisions in an interview project to a large extent come to rest on the integrity of the interviewer as a person.
- The ethical issues of an interview project go beyond the micro-ethics of protecting the interview subjects to also encompass macro-ethics concerning the value of the interview-produced knowledge in a larger social context.

31

Further reading

Ethical issues about and around doing interviews can be studied in reading the following texts:

Eisner, E.W. and Peshkin, A. (eds) (1990) *Qualitative Inquiry in Education.* New York: Teachers College Press.

Guidelines for the Protection of Human Subjects (1992). Berkeley: University of California Press.

Kimmel, A.J. (1988) *Ethics and Values in Applied Social Science Research.* Newbury Park, CA: Sage.

Mauthner, M., Birch, M., Jessop, J. and Miller, T. (eds) (2002) *Ethics in Qualitative Research.* Thousand Oaks, CA: Sage.

4
Planning an interview study

Seven stages of an interview inquiry   33
Thematizing an interview study   37
Designing an interview study   41
Mixed methods   46
Interviewing between method and craft   48

Chapter objectives
After reading this chapter, you should know

- more about the planning of an interview project;
- that the open structure of research interviewing is a strong as well as a problem field in interview;
- that an emotional account of potential hardships of an interview journey shows how things can go wrong when the overall design of an interview project is not taken into account;
- an idealized seven-stage route for an interview inquiry – thematizing, designing, interviewing, transcribing, analyzing, verifying and reporting;
- the pre-interview stages of thematizing and designing an interview project; and
- the tension of interviewing between method and craft.

Seven stages of an interview inquiry

The very virtue of qualitative interviews is their openness. No standard procedures or rules exist for conducting a research interview or an entire interview investigation. There are, however, standard choices of methods at the different stages of an interview investigation, and this chapter describes some of these choices. The aim is to enable the interview researcher to make decisions about method on a reflective level, based on knowledge of the topic of the study, the methodological options available, their ethical implications, and anticipated consequences of the choices for the entire interview project.

I shall here go beyond a dichotomy of all methods versus no method by focusing on the competence of the interview researcher. The quality of an interview study to a large extent rests on the craftsmanship of the researcher. The openness of the interview, with its many on-the-spot decisions – for example, whether to follow up new leads in an interview situation or to stick to the interview guide – puts strong demands on advance preparation and interviewer competence. The absence of a prescribed set of rules for interviewing creates an open-ended field of opportunity for the interviewer's skills, knowledge and intuition. Also, the design of an entire interview investigation follows fewer standard procedures than for example survey studies, where many of the method choices are already built into the standardized forms of questionnaires and the statistical analyses of the subjects' responses. The term 'unstandardized' pertains to the interview situation, but an entire interview investigation has often tended to be a rather standardized affair, going through five emotional phases of hardships.

Box 4.1   Emotional dynamics of an interview journey

Anti-positivist enthusiasm phase. An interview project may start with enthusiasm and commitment. The researcher is strongly engaged in a problem and wants to carry out realistic natural life research. It is to be meaningful qualitative research of people's lives, and not a positivist, quantified data gathering based on abstract theories.

The interview-quoting phase. By now the researcher will have recorded the initial interviews and is intensively engaged in the interviewees' stories. Forming a contrast to the ideological enthusiasm in the first phase, there is now personal involvement and a solitary identification with the subjects, who have revealed so much of their often oppressive life situation. At lunch the interviewer entertains his colleagues with a wealth of new quotations. Although exciting at first, it may after a while be difficult for the colleagues to remain fully involved in the myriad of interview stories.

The working phase of silence. After a time, silence falls upon the interview project. The researcher no longer brings up interview quotations at lunch. A colleague now asking about the project receives a laconic answer: 'The interviews are being transcribed' or 'The analysis has just started.' This working phase is characterized by sobriety and patience.

The aggressive phase of silence. A long time has passed since the interviews were completed and still no results have been presented. A colleague who now inquires about the project would run the risk of being met with distinct annoyance: the researcher bristles and more or less clearly signals: 'It's none of your business.' As for the researcher, this mid-project crisis is characterized by exceeded time limits, chaos, and stress.

(Continued)

(Continued)

The final phase of exhaustion. By now the interview project has become so overwhelming that there is hardly any time or energy left for reporting the originally interesting interview stories. One version of this phase is that 'nothing is reported' – the many hundred pages of transcribed interviews remain in the files. In a 'lecture version', the researcher conjures up some entertaining quotations in lectures, while the final report remains postponed. In a common 'save what can possibly be saved' termination, the interviews appear as isolated quotations in a report with little methodological and conceptual analyses. In cases where a more systematic 'final report' does appear, the researcher may feel resigned because he has not succeeded in passing on to the readers in a methodologically justifiable way the original richness of the interview stories.

Box 4.1 depicts the emotional dynamics of an interview journey. The descriptions are based upon observations of colleagues and students undertaking interview projects, as well as recollections from my own study of grading. The emotional intensity of the hardship phases varies. Moments of enthusiasm, common at the beginning, can also occur in the later phases, such as when discovering new meanings by reading the interview transcripts. It seldom happens, however, that the contrast between an initial enthusiasm and the later hardships is as distinct as in interview projects. However, the description of the hardships of an interview project was formulated some 25 years ago, at a time when interviewing was a relatively new method in the social sciences, with few conventions and little literature on interview research. The hardship tale may thus be less valid for interview research today.

Box 4.2   Seven stages of an interview inquiry

1. *Thematizing.* Formulate the purpose of an investigation and the conception of the theme to be investigated before the interviews start. The *why* and *what* of the investigation should be clarified before the question of *how* – method – is posed.
2. *Designing.* Plan the design of the study, taking into consideration all seven stages of the investigation, before interviewing (Chapter 4). Designing the study is undertaken with regard to obtaining the intended *knowledge* (Chapter 2) and taking into account the *moral* implications of the study (Chapter 3).
3. *Interviewing.* Conduct the interviews based on an interview guide and with a reflective approach to the knowledge sought and the interpersonal relation of the interview situation (Chapters 5, 6 and 7).

(Continued)

(Continued)

4. *Transcribing.* Prepare the interview material for analysis, which generally includes a transcription from oral speech to written text (Chapter 8).
5. *Analyzing.* Decide, on the basis of the purpose and topic of the investigation, and of the nature of the interview material, which modes of analysis are appropriate for the interviews (Chapter 9).
6. *Verifying.* Ascertain the validity, reliability and generalizability of the interview findings. Reliability refers to how consistent the results are, and validity means whether an interview study investigates what is intended to be investigated (Chapter 10).
7. *Reporting.* Communicate the findings of the study and the methods applied in a form that lives up to scientific criteria, takes the ethical aspects of the investigation into consideration and that results in a readable product (Chapter 11).

As a step towards invalidating the hardship tale, an interview investigation is outlined in Box 4.2 as a linear progression through seven stages from the original ideas to the final report. This idealized sequence may assist the interviewer through the potential hardships of a chaotic interview journey and contribute to retaining the initial vision and engagement throughout the investigation.

The emotional dynamics of an interview study are related to these seven stages. The anti-positivist enthusiasm dominates the usually quickly bypassed thematizing and designing. Engaged quoting covers the interviewing period. Quiet work and stress accompany transcription and analyzing. Verifying is often skipped, and exhaustion dominates the reporting of the study. The root of these ordeals is in the quick bypassing of the stages of thematizing and designing of an interview inquiry, addressed in this chapter.

Box 4.3   Seven stages of a grade study

1. *Thematizing.* Formulation of hypotheses about the influence of grading upon pupils on the basis of previous studies.
2. *Designing.* Planning the interviews with 30 high school pupils and 6 teachers.
3. *Interviewing.* A detailed guide was used for the individual interviews, each of which lasted about 45 minutes and was tape-recorded.

(Continued)

(Continued)

4.   *Transcribing.* All 36 pupil and teacher interviews were transcribed verbatim, resulting in about 1,000 pages of transcripts.
5.   *Analyzing.* The 30 pupil interviews were categorized with respect to different forms of grading behaviour. The interviews with the pupils and the teachers were also subjected to more extensive qualitative interpretations.
6.   *Verifying.* Reliability and validity checks were attempted throughout the project, including interviewer and scorer reliability, and validity of interpretations.
7.   *Reporting.* The results were reported in a book and in journal articles.

Source: Kvale (1980).

The slightly exaggerated hardship phases of an interview inquiry were to some extent based on my own interview study of grading in Danish high schools. Box 4.3 depicts post hoc, in an orderly fashion, the seven stages of the – at times – chaotic investigation of grades, which I will return to throughout this book.

Thematizing an interview study

A significant part of an interview project should take place before the tape recorder is turned on for the first actual interview. Thematizing refers to the formulation of research questions and a theoretical clarification of the theme investigated. The key questions when planning an interview investigation concern the why, what and how of the interview:

- *why*: clarifying the purpose of the study;
- *what*: obtaining a pre-knowledge of the subject matter to be investigated;
- *how*: becoming familiar with different techniques of interviewing and analyzing, and deciding which to apply to obtain the intended knowledge.

Method is here understood as the way to the goal. In order to find, or to show someone, the way to a goal, one needs to know what the goal is. It is necessary to identify the topic and the purpose of an interview investigation in order to make reflected decisions on which methods to use at the different stages on the way to the goal. Consultations on interview projects may sometimes take the form of an explorative 'counter'-interview. The counsellor first needs to explore, by carefully questioning the novice interviewer, where the interview journey is heading, what is the research topic of the interview study, and why it is undertaken, before the many technical questions about methods can be addressed. There is a standard reply to the method questions about design of qualitative interview studies – the answer depends on the purpose and the topic of the investigation. The thematic questions of 'why' and 'what' need to be answered before the technical 'how' questions of design can be posed and addressed meaningfully.

Research purpose

Thematizing an interview study involves clarifying the purpose of the study – the 'why'. Interviews may be conducted to obtain empirical knowledge of subjects' typical experiences of a topic. Or the interviews may seek knowledge of a social situation or of a life history, such as in biographical interviews, or of historical events. In the latter case of oral history interviews it is less the subject's experiences as such that are of interest, but the information they provide about social and historical events. The interviews may also go further than charting subjects' experiences, or using the subjects as informants about events, and attempt to get beyond the self-presentations of the subjects and critically examine the personal assumptions and general ideologies expressed in their statements.

Interviews can have explorative or hypothesis-testing purposes. An *exploratory* interview is usually open with little pre-planned structure. In this case the interviewer introduces an issue, an area to be charted or a problem complex to be uncovered, follows up on the subject's answers, and seeks new information about and new angles on the topic. Interviews that *test hypotheses* tend to be more structured. When investigating hypotheses about group differences, it may be preferable to standardize the wording and sequence of questions in order to compare the groups. Hypothesis testing can also take place within a single interview, where the interviewer questions to test out hypotheses about a subject's conception of an issue, such as in a confrontational interview by Bellah et al. about commitment and individualism (Box 6.3).

Interviews can also be primarily descriptive and seek to chart key aspects of the subject's lived world. They may further attempt to develop theoretical conceptions of a topic, such as in the grounded theory approach developed by Glaser and Strauss (1967), to *inductively* develop an empirically grounded theory through observations and interviews. An interview investigation may also seek to *deductively* test the implications of a theory. And interviews can be conducted in order to develop knowledge for, and throughout, collective activities in action research. Interviews are also used as *background material* for further practical and theoretical studies. Schön's (1987) analysis of the reflecting practitioner is thus based on interviews with professionals, and Sennett's (2004) book on respect builds on extensive interview experience.

Subject matter knowledge

Thematizing an interview study involves clarifying the theme of the study – the 'what'. This involves developing a conceptual and theoretical understanding of the phenomena to be investigated in order to establish the base to which new knowledge will be added and integrated. The thematic understanding of the topic of the study – the 'what' – will further provide a ground for the 'how' of the study: the many decisions on method that must be made on the way. Familiarity with the theme investigated is required to be able to pose significant questions, whether they concern the essence of beauty, truth and goodness in a Socratic dialogue, the strategy of a master chess player, or trends in rap music in a teenage interview.

Some interview investigations may start without a differentiated understanding or a theoretical conception of the themes to be investigated, and without a review of the research literature in the area. One definition of science is the systematic production of new knowledge. Without any presentation of the existing knowledge about the topic of an investigation, it is difficult for both researcher and reader to ascertain whether the knowledge obtained by the interviews is new, and thus what the scientific contribution of the research is. The theoretical naïveté of many current interview projects is not intrinsic to qualitative research. The contributions of Freud, as well as later psychotherapists, and of Piaget, testify to the potentials of theorizing on the basis of qualitative interviews. As more recent examples may be mentioned the studies of Hargreaves and Bourdieu (Boxes 1.2 and 1.3), in which the interviews were based upon, and served to develop, theoretical understanding.

The thematic focus of a project influences what aspects of a subject matter the questions centre upon, and which aspects remain in the background. The influence of differing theoretical conceptions upon choices of method may be exemplified by an imagined interview with a pupil about the *meaning of teasing*. Different psychological theories lead to different emphasis on emotions, experiences and behaviour, as well as on the temporal dimensions of past, present and future. Say a school psychologist is interviewing a pupil who, the teacher complains, is continually teasing the other pupils and thereby disturbing the class. The interview might be conducted from a Rogerian client-centred approach, a Freudian psychoanalytic approach and a Skinnerian behaviour-modification approach, respectively. Different kinds of interview questions are required to obtain the kinds of information necessary to interpret the meaning of teasing with respect to these theories. Simplified here, they would focus on present experiences and feelings about teasing, on family history and emotional dynamics, and on future behavioural consequences, such as the reactions of fellow pupils to the teasing, respectively. If these theoretical approaches, which highlight different aspects of the meaning of teasing, are not introduced until the analysis stage, the interviews may lack the relevant information for making specific interpretations on the basis of the different theories.

Familiarity with the content of an investigation is not obtained only through literature and theoretical studies. Just hanging out in the environment where the interviews are to be conducted will give an introduction to the local language, the daily routines and the power structures, and so provide a sense of what the interviewees will be talking about. Familiarity with the local situation may also sensitize to local ethico-political issues of the community, which need be taken into account when interviewing and reporting the interviews. Particularly for anthropological studies, a familiarity with the foreign culture is required for posing questions, as testified by the anthropologist Jean Lave:

> One of the reasons for doing field trips is that you are presented with how abstract is the most concrete of your concepts and questions when you are at home in the library. When I first went to Brazil I made my way 2,000 miles into north central Brazil and I arrived in a small town. I heard that there were Indians who actually were in town. And I can remember an incredible sense of excitement. I rushed out and walked around town until I found this group of Indians and walked straight up to them – and then I didn't know what to say. I wanted to ask: 'Have you got moiety systems?' (a special kind of kinship relations). And it didn't make sense to do that. In fact it took four months to find a way to ask a question with which I could discover from people whether they did have moiety systems. (Lave and Kvale, 1995, p. 221; slightly abbreviated)

Thematizing in the grade study

I shall now briefly report the thematizing of the study of grading in Danish high schools from 1978 (see Box 4.3 for the overall design). The study was instigated by a public debate about the effects of grading in connection with a new policy of restricted admission to college based on grade point averages from high school (Kvale, 1980). I had been involved in a newspaper debate with the Danish Minister of Education, who maintained that there would be hardly any educational or social impact from a restricted university admission based on grade point averages, and that contrary findings from other countries could not be generalized to the Danish situation. I decided to investigate the issue empirically by asking Danish pupils and teachers about their experiences with grading. Several hypotheses were formulated in advance. The first hypothesis of a grade perspective was: grading influences the process of learning and the social situation where learning occurs. A second hypothesis stated that the prevalence of the grading perspective would increase with a restricted admission to college based on grade point averages. The hypotheses were based on research literature, as discussed in my PhD dissertation on examinations and power (Kvale, 1972) and on later investigations of grading by other researchers.

Designing an interview study

Designing an interview study involves planning the procedures and techniques – the 'how' – of the study (Flick, 2007a). The following comments on formal designing pertain more to larger systematic interview investigations than to smaller flexible exploratory studies. A researcher familiar with the area of investigation and with interviewing may obtain important knowledge by more informal interview approaches.

Designing the grade study

I took special care to have a methodologically well-controlled design for the interviews about grades because their influence was a controversial public topic at the time, and I had a rather critical view of using the grade point average for selection to college. The use of qualitative interviews in research was also fairly new and contested at the time. Thirty high school pupils were interviewed individually about their experiences with grades. This number was a compromise between obtaining a representative sample and the resources available for the study. In order to counteract possible special circumstances at a single high school, the pupils were selected at random from three schools, one class in each. To counteract individual interviewer bias, the thirty pupils were distributed among four interviewers, three student assistants and myself. In order to gain an alternative perspective on the effects of grading, six teachers were also interviewed.

The temporal dimension of an interview design

The temporal dimension of an interview investigation should be kept in mind from the first thematizing to the final reporting stage, taking into account the interdependence of the seven stages. This includes having an overview of all seven stages of an interview study, paying attention to the interdependence of the stages and also pushing forward tasks at later stages – such as analysis and verification – to earlier stages, returning spirally to earlier stages, keeping the end point of the study in sight, and taking into account that the interviewer may become wiser throughout the study.

- *Overview*. A key factor of an interview inquiry is to develop an overview of the entire investigation before starting to interview. When using the more standardized methods, such as experiments, questionnaires and tests, the very structure of the instruments requires advance decisions about the way in which the study will be conducted. In this case, methodological alternatives are already built into the instruments, for instance by the response alternatives of questionnaires and by computer programs for statistical analysis and presentation of the numerical findings. In open and non-standardized interview studies, however, the choices of method may first appear during the investigation, in some cases when it is too late to make decisions appropriate for the topic and purpose of the study.

- *Interdependence*. There are strong interconnections among the choices of method made at the different stages. A decision at one stage has consequences that both open and limit the alternatives available at the next stage. For example, a statistical generalization of the findings of an interview study to larger groups will require that certain criteria – regarding size and representativeness of the sample of subjects – are taken into account already by selection of interviewees. And if the researcher wants to make a systematic linguistic or conversational analysis of the interviews, this would not be possible or would require a time-consuming re-transcription, if the interviews had been edited into normal English by the transformation from oral to written language.

- *Push forward*. Attempt to do much of the work of the post-interview stages at earlier stages. Although the problems of an interview project tend to surface in the analysis stage, more often than not they originate in earlier stages. The solution is to improve the quality of the original interviews. Thus, clarifying the meanings of statements during an interview will make the later analysis easier and more well founded; asking control questions during the interview will facilitate the validation of interpretations. Improving interview quality is not simply a question of better interview techniques; it also involves a reflective thematization of the topic and purpose of the inquiry from the very beginning.

- *Spiralling backwards*. An interview project is often characterized by a back-and-forth process between different stages. The linear progression of the seven stages discussed here may in practice be modified into a circular or spiral model where the researcher, with an extended understanding of the themes investigated, at later stages returns to earlier stages. This may be to make extra interviews, to re-transcribe specific passages, or to reanalyze the interview stories from new perspectives.

- *Keep the end point in sight*. From the start of the investigation, keep the expected result in view. Is the intended outcome a PhD thesis or an internal evaluation report? Will a publication result from the study? As a short article or as a book? For a scientific forum or for the general public? The answers to such questions should serve as guidelines throughout the stages of the interview project, assisting the informed decisions made on the way and keeping the project on track towards the goal. The nature of the final report is decisive for decisions at earlier stages on such ethical issues as: informing the interviewees about later use of what they say, obtaining written permission to quote extensively from their interviews, and judging how personal themes can be addressed in interviews intended for public use.

- *Getting wiser*. An interviewer may learn throughout an investigation. The conversations with the subjects can extend and alter his or her understanding of the phenomena investigated. The interviewees bring forth new and unexpected aspects of the phenomena studied, and during analysis of the transcribed interviews new distinctions may be discovered. This is well in line with the purpose of an exploratory study – to discover new dimensions of the research topic. In comparative hypothesis-testing studies, however, it may create design problems if the interviewer continually obtains new significant insights. Novel dimensions of a phenomenon may be discovered in the middle of a series of interviews testing, for example, the influence of grades upon girl and boy ways of learning a school subject. The dilemma will then be whether to improve the interview guide with specific questions to the new dimensions in the remainder of the interviews, and not have comparable groups, or to refrain from using the new insights in the remaining interviews. No easy solution to the dilemma of becoming wiser as a threat to standardized conditions is offered, except to be as clear as possible about the main purposes of a study from its inception. Thus in exploratory studies the questioning may continually improve as the researcher learns more about a topic, ideally resulting in a sophisticated interviewing sensitive to the nuances and complexities of the topic explored.
- *Work-journal*. In order to keep track of the temporal vicissitudes of an interview journey, the researcher can keep a work-journal as a record of his or her learning throughout the investigation. The daily insights obtained by the construction of interview knowledge are noted down, including changed understandings of previous experiences, as well as reflections on the research process. During analysis, verification and reporting, the work-journal will then provide the researcher with a frame for understanding and reflecting on processes and changes of the knowledge production throughout an interview inquiry.

How many interview subjects do I need?

To the common question about interview inquiries, 'How many interview subjects do I need?', the answer is simply: 'Interview as many subjects as necessary to find out what you need to know.' In qualitative interview studies, the number of subjects tends to be either too small or too large. If the number of subjects is too small, it is difficult to generalize and not possible to test hypotheses of differences among groups or to make statistical generalizations. If the number of subjects is too large, there will hardly be time to make penetrating analyses of the interviews.

The number of subjects necessary depends on the purpose of a study. If the aim is to understand the world as experienced by one specific person, say in a biographical interview, this one subject is sufficient. If the intention is to explore and describe in detail the attitudes of boys and girls towards grades, new interviews might be conducted until a point of saturation, where further interviews yield little new knowledge. If the goal is to predict the outcome of a national election, a representative sample of about 1,000 subjects is normally required, so qualitative interviews are out of the question, and questionnaires are used. If the purpose is to statistically test hypotheses about different attitudes of boys and girls towards competition for grades, the necessary sample may be as small as 3 boys and 3 girls. Depending on the distribution of the findings, a Fisher test of significant differences between the two groups of three can be made at a probability level of $p < 0.05$ (Siegel, 1956). In common interview studies, the amount of interviews tends to be around 15 ± 10. This number may be due to a combination of the time and resources available for the investigation and a law of diminishing returns. A general impression from current interview studies is that many would have profited from having fewer interviews in the study, and by taking more time to prepare the interviews and to analyze them. Perhaps as a defensive overreaction, some qualitative interview studies appear to be designed on a quantitative presupposition – the more interviews, the more scientific.

I shall here draw on the grade study to illustrate the issue of the number of subjects and also the use of mixed methods optimizing the strong points of interviews and questionnaires. In the interview passage presented in Chapter 1, a pupil asserted a connection between pupils' talkativeness and their grades. In a follow-up study by two of my students, the statement was split into two items in a questionnaire (Hvolbøl and Kristensen, 1983). Table 4.1 presents the percentage of agreement among 239 pupils from 6 schools when the interview statement from Chapter 1 was converted into a questionnaire form. It turned out that a clear majority of the pupils agreed with the first part of the statement of the pupil interviewed – that grades are an expression of how much one talks – whereas a majority disagreed with the second part – that grades are often an expression of how much one goes along with the teacher's opinion. With the large number of subjects the questionnaire could then check the generality of the views stated by one pupil, a generality that would require too many resources to test by the more time-demanding qualitative interviews. In retrospect, the grade study would probably have produced more valuable knowledge with fewer, but longer, more intensive interviews and by subjecting them to more penetrating interpretations. The questionnaire developed later on the basis of the interviews could then have tested the generality of the interview findings.

This example points to strengths and weaknesses of interviews and questionnaires. The interview brought out interesting beliefs about which behaviours lead to good grades, whereas the questionnaire made it possible to test how prevalent these beliefs were among a large number of pupils. While the interviewer could closely question the strength of a pupil's belief, and might also have obtained concrete examples supporting the claims, the questionnaire used did not follow up the pupils' statements. In the present approach there are no important

TABLE 4.1   From interview statements to questionnaire items

Interview Statement
Pupil: Grades are often unjust, because very often – very often – they are only a measure of how much you talk, and how much you agree with the teacher's opinion.

Questionnaire items	Percentage of 239 pupils			
	Strongly agree	Agree	Disagree	Strongly disagree
Grades are often an expression of how much one talks in class	20	62	15	3
Grades are often an expression of how much one follows the teacher's opinion	4	20	57	19

epistemological differences between mixing the methods of interviews and questionnaires; they merely provide answers to different kinds of research questions, namely, of what kind of beliefs the pupils have of grades and of how many pupils have these kinds of beliefs.

When not to interview

In this chapter on interview design it may be pertinent also to mention some areas and uses for which qualitative interviews are little suited. One purpose of the present book is to lead some readers *away* from using research interviews, by pointing out that in several cases other methods may be more appropriate for the subject matter and purpose of the intended research.

If a study seeks to predict the behaviour of larger groups, such as voting behaviour, larger samples of respondents are necessary than would be possible to cover with time-consuming qualitative interviews; in such cases, survey questionnaires with pre-coded answers are the relevant method. Also, when there is little time available for a project, questionnaires will usually be faster to administer, analyze and report than qualitative interviews.

If you want to study people's behaviour and their interaction with their environment, the observations and informal conversations of field studies will usually give more valid knowledge than merely asking subjects about their behaviour. If the research topic concerns more implicit meanings and tacit understandings, like the taken-for-granted assumptions of a group or a culture, then participant observation and field studies of actual behaviour supplemented by informal interviews may give more valid information.

If the purpose of a study is to obtain penetrating personal knowledge of a subject, then this may best be obtained through the trust developed in the close, personal interaction developed through a long and emotional therapy process (cf. Box 2.3). Whereas the challenges to a person's established self-image and the provoking of strong feelings are necessary parts of therapy, inciting such intensive emotional reactions only for research interests would be unethical.

When planning an interview study, it may thus be appropriate to consider whether other methods may be better suitable for the theme and purpose of the project. This being said, it should not be forgotten that interviews are particularly suited for studying people's understanding of the meanings in their lived world, describing their experiences and self-understanding, and clarifying and elaborating their own perspective on their lived world.

Mixed methods

Today the use of 'mixed methods' has become a controversial theme, in particular the combination of qualitative and quantitative methods with allegedly different paradigmatic assumptions. The controversy has become embedded in the socio-political context of the social sciences, where a methodological hierarchy is often implied, with quantitative methods at the top and qualitative methods relegated to a largely auxiliary role (Howe, 2004).

Somehow the use of mixed methods, or their allegedly paradigmatic differences, was not an issue in the historical interview studies mentioned earlier. Thus Piaget's investigations of children's thought were a free combination of observations, quasi-naturalistic experiments and interviews. The study of the authoritarian personality by Adorno et al., originating from psychoanalytic interviews, used a sophisticated interplay of open qualitative interviews and highly structured questionnaires for producing and validating data. The many thousand interviews in the Hawthorne study were conducted to find out why production continued to increase with experimental changes in the worker's conditions and how human relations could be improved in the factories. In current marketing research, a combination of focus group interviews and questionnaires is a matter of course when introducing a new product.

In social science research today, interviews are frequently used in combination with other methods. Thus Bourdieu's investigations of social selection and marginalization in the educational system and of social oppression in France combined an extensive use of quantitative and qualitative approaches. Interviews are often applied in *case studies,* which focus on a specific person, situation or institution. Interviews can also serve as an *auxiliary method* in conjunction with other methods. By participant observation and in ethnographic field studies, more or less informal interviews are therefore important sources of information. At the construction of questionnaires it is common to use pilot interviews to chart the main aspects of a topic and also test how survey questions are understood. In post-experimental interviews, subjects are questioned on how they understood the experimental design.

In the present pragmatic approach, the different methods are different tools for answering different questions; qualitative methods refer to what kind, and quantitative methods to how much of a kind. In the present perspective, the important issues by the use of mixed methods are less on a paradigmatic level than on a socio-political level about whether qualitative knowledge is scientific as well as at a practical level. Thus, to work with different media – words and numbers – and to manage questionnaire construction and statistical analyses, as well as interviewing forms and analytic techniques, all at a high quality level, each demands expertise obtained through long training.

Resources and expertise

At the start of a project the resources and the expertise necessary for an interview study can be easily overlooked. Relevant questions about resources are: How much time does the researcher have available for the study? Is there any money available for assistance – for example, for transcribing the interviews? Usually, conducting the interviews themselves is not time-consuming whereas transcribing them requires much more time, and assistance for transcription may be expensive. The subsequent analysis of the transcripts is usually the most time-consuming part of the interview study.

With the closeness to the everyday conversations we are so familiar with, research interviewing may appear easy, as something everyone with a minimal introduction can undertake. The interviewer poses some simple questions, records and transcribes the interview, and hopes that a computer program will take care of finding meaning in the interviews. This kind of interview research may become a 'research light', with little probability of producing substantial new knowledge.

Rigorous interview training is not commonplace in social science methodology programs today. A weekend course and an introductory interview textbook may be considered sufficient to embark on a PhD project based on interviews. In contrast, in several professional contexts, intensive training of the interviewers may be required. Authorization to conduct psychoanalytic interviews requires years of training. In the Hawthorne investigations of human relations in industry, several years of training were considered necessary to become a proficient interviewer. For focus group interviews in consumer research, Chrzanowska (2002) has estimated about two years' training to be necessary for becoming a qualified focus group moderator.

I shall return to the practical training for interviewing and outline an 'interview practicum' in Chapter 12. We may conclude here that there is a paradox of strong demands on training professional therapeutic and commercial interviewers and comparatively little emphasis on the training of academic interview researchers for producing scientific knowledge.

Interviewing between method and craft

A priority of method has loomed large in modern social science. Also in current interview research there has been an emphasis on methods of interviewing and, in particular, on methods for analyzing the transcribed interviews. Method may be understood in a broad sense, following the original Greek meaning of the term as the way to a goal. In positivist and analytic approaches to the social sciences, however, method has become restricted to a mechanical rule-following, for example: 'A method is a set of rules, which can be used in a mechanical way to realize a given aim. The mechanical element is important: a method shall not presuppose judgment, artistic or other creative abilities', (Elster, 1980, p. 295).

Within such a formal rule conception of method, the qualitative research interview, where knowledge is produced through the personal interaction between interviewer and interviewee, is clearly not a scientific method. In the bureaucratic conception of method the ideal interview would be an interviewer-free method. A contrasting approach of emphasizing the person of the researcher as the very research instrument has been advocated by some social researchers, for example by the anthropologist Jean Lave in the following interview sequence:

> **SK**: Is there an anthropological method? If yes, what is an anthropological method?
>
> **JL**: I think it is complete nonsense to say that we have a method. First of all I don't think that anyone should have *a* method. But in the sense that there are 'instruments' that characterize the 'methods' of different disciplines – sociological surveys, questionnaire methods, in psychology various kinds of tests and also experiments – there are some very specific technical ways of inquiring into the world. Anthropologists refuse to take those as proper ways to study human beings. I think the most general view is that the only instrument that is sufficiently complex to comprehend and learn about human existence is another human. And so what you use is your own life and your own experience in the world. (Lave and Kvale, 1995, p. 220)

When the person of the researcher is conceived as the main research instrument, this entails an emphasis upon the competence and craftsmanship – the skills, sensitivity and knowledge – of the researcher. With craftsmanship I refer to mastery of a form of production, which requires practical skills and personal insight acquired through training and extensive practice. In a discussion of validation of qualitative research, Mishler has argued that researchers turn out to resemble practitioners of a craft more than logicians. Their competence depends upon contextual knowledge of the specific methods applicable to a phenomenon of interest: 'Skilled research is a craft, and like any craft, it is learned by apprenticeship to competent researchers, by hands-on experience, and by continual practice' (Mishler, 1990, p. 422). We may add that also in biographies of Nobel laureates in the natural sciences a craftsman-like understanding of research may go forth with an emphasis on research training through apprenticeships in scientific laboratories (cf. Kvale, 1997).

The present approach emphasizes interviewing as a craft. Interview practice does not follow content- and context-free rules of method, but rests on the judgements of a qualified researcher. The interviewer is the research instrument, and the quality of the knowledge produced in an interview depends on the skills, the sensitivity and the subject matter knowledge of the interviewer. The relation of the interview to the survey questionnaire and therapy can again be drawn in. Because there are explicit rules for administering standardized questionnaires, new interviewers can be fully trained in a matter of hours or days. In contrast, the qualifications for conducting a research interview on a professional level require extensive training, and for a psychoanalytic interview years of academic and therapeutic training are required.

Knowledge of interviewing is less embedded in explicit rules of method than in concrete examples of interviews. The proficient craftsman does not focus on the methods but on the task – in Heidegger's analysis of craftwork it is not the hammer the carpenter focuses on, but on the wood and the table to be built. Learning to interview is to arrive at a transparency of the techniques and tools. The proficient interviewer thinks less of interviewing technique than of the interviewee and the knowledge sought.

Substantial familiarity with the theme and context of an inquiry is a precondition for the expert interviewing. Method as rule-following is in research interviewing replaced by the researcher's expert knowledge of the theme to be investigated and by mastery of the techniques of an interview inquiry. Good interview research goes beyond knowledge of formal rules and encompasses more than mastering the technical skills of a craft, to also include a personal judgement about which rules and techniques to invoke or not invoke. Formal apprenticeship in a trade where students learn interviewing in the interaction of research communities with masters of the craft is not commonly available. When the option is to be self-taught, a manual in a book form may be better than nothing.

===== **Key points**

- The open nature of the interview situation promotes production of new knowledge, but may entail problems at later systematic comparison and analysis of the interviews.

- Taking account from the start of all seven stages of an interview journey can alleviate some of its hardships and contribute to producing interview knowledge of a higher quality. These stages are thematizing, designing, interviewing, transcribing, analyzing, verifying and reporting.
- The more attention is given to the pre-interview stages of thematizing and analyzing, the higher the likelihood of producing high-quality interviews. And the higher the interview quality, the easier will be the post-interview stages of transcribing, analyzing, verifying and reporting the interviews, and the more likely it is that an interview inquiry will lead to significant new knowledge.
- Interviewing may be regarded less as a method following explicit rules than pragmatically as a craft, where the quality of knowledge produced by the interview rests upon the subject matter knowledge and the craftsmanship of the interviewer.

Further reading

Issues of research design for interview studies and qualitative research in general are outlined in these publications:

Flick, U. (2007a) *Designing Qualitative Research* (Book 1 of *The SAGE Qualitative Research Kit*). London: Sage.
Marshall, C. and Rossman, G.B. (2006) *Designing Qualitative Research* (4th ed.). Thousands Oaks, CA: Sage.

5
Conducting an interview

A class interview about grades   52
Setting the interview stage   55
Scripting the interview   56
Interviewer questions   60
The art of second questions   63

Chapter objectives
After reading this chapter you should understand

- the process of producing knowledge through an interview;
- from a demonstration interview the interaction and the questioning in the interview;
- the preparations for an interview, such as setting the stage for the interview and preparing a script in the form of an interview guide; and
- the role of researcher questions, interviewer questions, the linguistic forms of questions and the art of second questions.

This chapter does not lead to any general rules for interviewing, but describes some of the techniques of the interview craft, techniques to be learned through extensive practice. With the techniques of interviewing mastered, the interviewer may concentrate on the subject and the subject matter of the interview. In this chapter I treat semi-structured life-world interviews, and in the following chapter I present an overview of a variety of interview forms. The semi-structured life-world interview seeks to obtain descriptions of the life-world of the interviewee with respect to interpreting the meaning of the described phenomenon; it will have a sequence of themes to be covered, as well as some suggested questions. Yet at the same time there is openness to changes of sequence and forms of questions in order to follow up the specific answers given and the stories told by the subjects. The open phenomenological approach of a life-world interview to learning from the interviewee is well expressed in this introduction to anthropological interviewing:

> I want to understand the world from your point of view. I want to know what you know in the way you know it. I want to understand the meaning of your experience, to walk in your shoes, to feel things as you feel them, to explain things as you explain them. Will you become my teacher and help me understand? (Spradley, 1979, p. 34)

A class interview about grades

Below follows an interview (see Box 5.1) that I conducted before a class at an interview workshop at Saybrook Institute, San Francisco, in 1987. Although the interview situation is artificial, it gives in a condensed form a fair picture of a semi-structured life-world interview. The interview is reproduced shortened and verbatim, with only a few minor changes in linguistic style.

Box 5.1   Demonstration interview

Steinar Kvale 0: I will now attempt to demonstrate the mode of understanding in a qualitative research interview, and I need a volunteer. It will be a rather neutral topic, it's not a psychoanalytic depth interview. The interview will take about ten minutes and afterwards we will discuss it here.

A woman in her thirties volunteers.

SK 1: Thank you for your willingness to participate and be interviewed here. I have been studying the effects of grades in Europe for some years, and now I'm interested in the meaning of grades for American students and pupils. I want to first ask you a maybe difficult question. If you'll try to remember back when you went to primary school, are you able to remember the first time you ever had any grades?

Student 1: I remember a time; but it might not have been the first time.

SK 2: Let's take that time. Can you tell me what happened?

Student 2: I did very well. I remember getting a red star on the top of my paper with 100; and that stands out in my memory as exciting and interesting.

SK 3: Yes. Is it only the red star that stands out, or what happened around it?

(Continued)

(Continued)

Student 3: (laughter) I remember the colour very very well. It was shining. I remember getting rewarded all the way around. I remember being honoured by my classmates and the teacher and my parents – them making a fuss. And some of the other kids not responding so well who didn't do so well. It was mixed emotions, but generally I remember the celebration aspect.

SK 4: You said mixed emotions. Are you able to describe them?

Student 4: Well, at that time I was the teacher's pet and some people would say, 'Aha, maybe she didn't earn it, maybe it's just because the teacher likes her so well.' And some kind of stratification occurring because I was not only the teacher's pet but I was maybe getting better grades and it created some kind of dissonance within my classmates' experience of me socially.

SK 5: Could you describe that dissonance?

Student 5: Well, I think there's always some kind of demarcation between students who do well and students who don't do as well, and that's determined, especially in the primary grades, by the number that you get on top of your paper.

SK 6: Was this early in school? Was it first grade?

Student 6: Third grade.

SK 7: Third grade. Well, that's a long time ago. Are you able to remember what they said? Or –

Student 7: No; it was more the feeling –

SK 8: The feeling –

Student 8: Yeah, it was the feeling of, I'd put some space between me and the peer group –

SK 9: Because of your good grades -

Student 9: Yeah.

SK 10: Did you try to do anything about that?

Student 10: I didn't do so well after that. It really affected me in a large way. I wanted to be with them more than I wanted to be with the teacher, or on the teacher's good list. So it was significant.

SK 11: It was a significant experience – (Yes) – to you, and you got in a conflict between teacher and your peers, or you experienced it as a conflict. (Yes) Did your parents enter into the situation?

Student 11: Not that I recall, because it was – to me it was a significant alteration in how I experienced grades. To them it was maybe just a little bit less. But it was still satisfactory, still acceptable, and I was still rewarded in general terms for doing well and not failing. So that dichotomy was respected.

(Continued)

(Continued)

SK 12: That kind of dissonance between say loyalty to your teacher and the affection of the classmates, is that a situation you have been into other times? Does it remind you of – other – ?

Student 12: It keeps repeating itself in my life, yes. Whenever I start taking my friends or my peer group for granted, I get some kind of message saying, Huh-uh, what's more important to me? And what's more important to me is my friendships.

SK 13: Um-hmm. That is the basic issue. You mentioned several times before 'rewarded' – what do you mean by 'rewarded'?

Student 13: Oh, getting to stay up to watch TV when I was in third grade, maybe; or getting to go some place or stay out later or maybe just getting ice-cream, some food –

(The remainder of the interview, omitted here for reasons of space, went on about the importance of the student's friendships in college, and it ended as follows:)

SK 26: Okay – Are there any more things you would want to say before we end the interview?

Student 26: No, I don't think so.

SK 27: Okay; thank you very much for your cooperation.

(The interview was then discussed in class, including the following exchange:)

SK 28: How did you experience being interviewed about it (the grades) up in front here?

Student 28: I thought it was a really good opportunity for me to explore that. I haven't even thought about it in a long time, but I knew from therapy that I've had recently that was a big time in my life when I was closer to my teacher than I was to my friends and I've had to face that a lot. It was fun for me to talk about it 'cause I'm pretty clear about what happened.

When we look at the knowledge brought forth in this short interview passage, several important aspects of the social effects of grading are manifested, primarily a pervasive loyalty conflict between teacher and friends; being a teacher's pet getting high grades created a dissonance in her classmates' experiences of her, it put a space between her and the peer group, a dissonance that kept repeating itself in her life, with her friendships being the most important (Student 3–5).

The mode of producing knowledge in this interview was inspired by Rogers's client-centred questioning. Thematically, I had, in the interview guide, wanted to address meanings of grading from three theoretical positions mentioned earlier – a Rogerian, a Freudian and a Skinnerian approach (Chapter 4). Thus, when the student described 'mixed emotions' (3) and 'it was more the feeling' (7), I sought, in line with a Rogerian approach, to encourage further elaboration of the feeling and the mixed emotions by repeating these very words (SK 4 and 8). A Freudian approach in a broad sense was tried by asking, 'Did your parents enter into the situation?' (SK 11) and, later, whether the loyalty conflict between teacher and pupils reminded her of other situations (SK 12). The student's answer confirms that this keeps repeating itself in her life, but she does not bring up family relations. I here had in mind her grade-loyalty conflict as possibly reactivating childhood conflicts of jealousy and sibling rivalry for the affection of parents. Early in the interview the student (3) had mentioned reinforcements for good grades, such as being honoured by her classmates, teacher and parents. I pursued a Skinnerian reinforcement approach (SK 13) by probing the meaning of the student's term 'rewarded' (3 and 13). The student then tells about being rewarded for good grades as a child by getting to stay up late to watch TV or by being given ice-cream (13).

Setting the interview stage

The setting of the interview stage should encourage the interviewees to describe their points of view on their lives and worlds. The first minutes of an interview are decisive. The interviewees will want to have a grasp of the interviewer before they allow themselves to talk freely and expose their experiences and feelings to a stranger. A good contact is established by attentive listening, with the interviewer showing interest, understanding and respect for what the subject says, and with an interviewer at ease and clear about what he or she wants to know.

The interview is introduced by a *briefing* in which the interviewer defines the situation for the subject, briefly tells about the purpose of the interview, the use of a tape recorder, and so on, and asks if the subject has any questions before starting the interview. Further information can preferably wait until the interview is over. The demonstration interview about grades was introduced with a briefing about the purpose and context of the interview before (SK 0) and at the start of the interview (SK 1).

At the end of an interview there may be some tension or anxiety, because the subject has been open about often personal and emotional experiences and may be wondering about the purpose and later use of the interview. There may perhaps also be feelings of emptiness; the subject has given much information about his or her life and may not have received anything in return. This being said, a common experience after research interviews is that the subjects have experienced the interview as genuinely enriching, have enjoyed talking freely with an attentive listener and have sometimes obtained new insights into important themes of their life world.

The initial briefing should be followed up by a *debriefing* after the interview. The demonstration interview was thus rounded off by a debriefing: before ending the interview by asking if the student had anything more to say (SK 26), and also after the interview by asking her about her experience of the interview (SK 28), an invitation she accepted when commenting further on the interview theme in relation to her biography.

An interview may also be rounded off with the interviewer mentioning some of the main points he or she has learned from the interview. The subject might then want to comment on this feedback. After this the interaction may be concluded by the interviewer saying, for example, 'I have no further questions. Is there anything else you would like to bring up, or ask about, before we finish the interview?' This gives the subject an additional opportunity to deal with issues he or she has been thinking or worrying about during the interview. The debriefing is likely to continue after the tape recorder has been turned off. After a first gasp of relief, some interviewees may then bring up topics that they did not feel safe raising with the tape recorder on. And the interviewer can now, insofar as the subject is interested, tell more about the purpose and design of the interview study.

The live interview situation, with the interviewee's voice and facial and bodily expressions accompanying the statements, provides a richer access to the subjects' meanings than the transcribed texts will do later on. It may be worthwhile for the interviewer to set aside 10 minutes or more of quiet time after each interview to reflect on what has been learned from the particular interview. These immediate impressions, based on the interviewer's empathetic access to the meanings communicated in the live interview interaction, may – in the form of notes or simply recorded onto the interview tape – provide a valuable context for the later analysis of transcripts.

If an interview is to be reported, perhaps quoted at length, then an attempt should be made when feasible to make the social context explicit during the interview, and also the emotional tone of the interaction, so that what is said is understandable to the readers, who have not witnessed the lived bodily presence of the interview situation. Much is to be learned from journalists and novelists about how to use questions and replies to also convey the setting and mood of a conversation.

Scripting the interview

The interview stage is usually prepared with a script. An interview guide is a script that structures the course of the interview more or less tightly. The guide may merely contain some topics to be covered or it can be a detailed sequence of carefully worded questions. For the semi-structured type of interview discussed here, the guide will include an outline of topics to be covered, with suggested questions. It will depend on the particular study whether the questions and their sequence are strictly predetermined and binding on the interviewers, or whether it is up to an interviewer's judgement and tact how closely to stick to the guide and how much to follow up the interviewees' answers and the new directions they may open up.

Interviews differ in their openness of purpose; the interviewer can explain the purpose and pose direct questions from the start, or can adopt a roundabout approach, with indirect questions, and reveal the purpose only when the interview is over. The latter approach is called a funnel-shaped interview – an interviewer interested in exploring religious attitudes in a community may start by asking generally about the neighbourhood, go on to ask if there are many immigrants, to end up specifically asking about attitudes to their Moslem neighbours. The application of such indirect interview techniques needs to be considered in relation to the ethical guidelines of informed consent.

An interview question can be evaluated with respect to both a thematic and a dynamic dimension: thematically with regard to producing knowledge, and dynamically with regard to the interpersonal relationship in the interview. A good interview question should contribute thematically to knowledge production and dynamically to promoting a good interview interaction.

Thematically the questions relate to the 'what' of an interview, to the theoretical conceptions of the research topic, and to the subsequent analysis of the interview. The questions will differ when interviewing for spontaneous descriptions of the lived world, interviewing for coherent narratives, or interviewing for a conceptual analysis of the person's understanding of a topic. The more spontaneous the interview procedure, the more likely one is to obtain spontaneous, lively and unexpected answers from the interviewees. And on the other hand, the more structured the interview situation is, the easier the later conceptual structuring of the interview by analysis will be.

In line with the principle of 'pushing forward', the later stage of interview analysis should be taken into account when preparing the interview questions. If the analysis is to involve coding the answers, then continually during the interview clarify the meanings of the answers with respect to the categories to be used later. If a narrative analysis is to be employed, then give the subjects ample freedom and time to unfold their own stories, and follow up with questions to shed light on the main episodes and characters in their narratives.

Dynamically the questions pertain to the 'how' of an interview; they should promote a positive interaction, keep the flow of the conversation going, and stimulate the subjects to talk about their experiences and feelings. The questions should be easy to understand, short, and devoid of academic language. A conceptually good thematic research question need not be a good dynamic interview question. Novice interviewers may be tempted to start with direct conceptual questions. The sociologist Sennett thus received the following response when as a young student he used a rather direct approach when interviewing members of the Boston elite: "'My what, young man?' an elderly Boston matron replied when I asked her, point-blank over tea in the Sommerset Club, to describe her identity. I had just made the tyro interviewer's error of assuming that frontal attack is the best way to elicit information from others' (Sennett, 2004, p. 41).

When preparing an interview, it may be useful to develop two interview guides, one with the project's thematic research questions and the other with interview questions to be posed, which takes both the thematic and the dynamic dimensions into account. The researcher questions are usually formulated in a theoretical language, whereas the interviewer questions should be expressed in the everyday language of the interviewees. Table 5.1 depicts the translation of thematic research questions in the grading study into interview questions that could provide thematic knowledge and also contribute dynamically to a natural conversational flow. The academic research questions, such as those about intrinsic and extrinsic motivation, need to be translated into an easy-going, colloquial form to generate spontaneous and rich descriptions. The abstract wording of the research questions would hardly lead to off-the-cuff answers from high school pupils. One research question can be investigated through several interview questions, thus obtaining rich and varied information by approaching a topic from several angles. And one interview question might provide answers to several research questions (see also Flick, 2007a, chap. 2).

The roles of the 'why', 'what' and 'how' questions differ in the case of research questions and interview questions. When designing an interview project, the 'why' and 'what' questions should be asked and answered before the question of 'how' is posed. In the interview situation, the priority changes; here the main questions should be in a descriptive form: 'What happened and how did it happen?', 'How did you feel then?', 'What did you experience?' and the like. The aim is to elicit spontaneous descriptions from the subjects rather than to get their own, more or less speculative explanations of why something took place. Many 'why' questions in an interview may lead to an over-reflected intellectualized interview, and perhaps also evoke memories of oral examinations. Figuring out the reasons and explanations why something happened is primarily the task of the investigator. 'Why' questions about the subjects' own reasons for their actions may nevertheless be important in their own right, and when posed, then preferably towards the end of the interview.

The question of why the subjects experience and act as they do is primarily a task for the researcher to evaluate, and the interviewer may here go beyond the subjects' self-understanding. An analogy to a doctor's diagnosis may be clarifying. The doctor does not start by asking the patient why he or she is sick,

TABLE 5.1   Research questions and interview questions

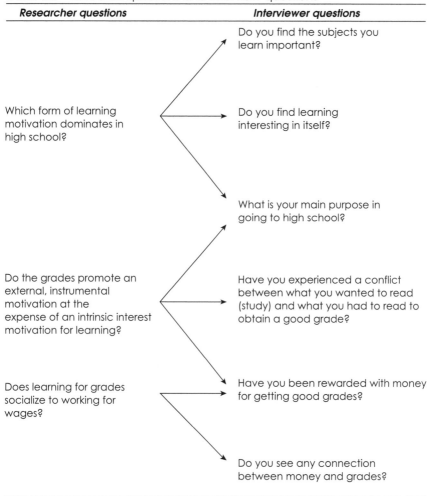

Researcher questions	Interviewer questions
Which form of learning motivation dominates in high school?	Do you find the subjects you learn important?
	Do you find learning interesting in itself?
	What is your main purpose in going to high school?
Do the grades promote an external, instrumental motivation at the expense of an intrinsic interest motivation for learning?	Have you experienced a conflict between what you wanted to read (study) and what you had to read to obtain a good grade?
Does learning for grades socialize to working for wages?	Have you been rewarded with money for getting good grades?
	Do you see any connection between money and grades?

but rather asks the patient what is wrong, what he or she is feeling and what the symptoms are. On the basis of the information from the patient interview, and from other methods of investigation, the doctor then makes a diagnosis of which illness is likely. For both the doctor and the researcher there are cases where it is important to know the subject's own explanations of his or her condition and to ask questions about why. The primary task for both the doctor and the interview researcher, however, remains that of obtaining descriptions so that they will have relevant and reliable material from which to draw their interpretations.

In addition to paying attention to the thematic and dynamic aspects of the questions, the interviewer should also try to keep in mind the later analysis, verification and reporting of the interviews. Interviewers who know what they are asking about and why they are asking, will attempt to clarify the meanings relevant to the project during the interview. Such attempts at disambiguation of interviewees' statements will provide a more secure ground for the later analysis. These efforts of meaning clarification during the interview may also communicate to the subject that the researcher is actually listening to, and interested in, what he or she is saying. Ideally the testing of hypotheses and of interpretations is finished at the end of the interview, with the interviewer's hypotheses and interpretations verified, falsified or refined.

Interviewer questions

The interviewer's questions should be brief and simple. The introductory question may concern a concrete situation; thus I opened the demonstration interview with a question of whether the student remembered the first time she ever had any grades (SK 1). The dimensions of grading introduced in her answer were then followed up in the remainder of the interview.

The interview researcher is his or her own research tool. The interviewer's ability to sense the immediate meaning of an answer, and the horizon of possible meanings that it opens up, is decisive. This, again, requires a knowledge of and interest in the research theme and the human interaction of the interview, as well as familiarity with modes of questioning, in order that the interviewer can devote his or her attention to the interview subject and the interview topic.

Box 5.2 Interview questions

A. *Introductory questions.* 'Can you tell me about ... ?'; 'Do you remember an occasion when ... ?'; 'What happened in the episode you mentioned?'; and 'Could you describe in as much detail as possible a situation in which learning occurred for you?' Such opening questions may yield spontaneous, rich descriptions where the subjects themselves provide what they experience as the main aspects of the phenomenon investigated.

B. *Follow-up questions.* The subjects' answers may be extended through a curious, persistent and critical attitude of the interviewer. This can be done

(Continued)

(Continued)

through direct questioning of what has just been said. Also a mere nod, or 'mm', or just a pause can invite the subject to go on with the description. Repeating significant words of an answer can lead to further elaboration. Interviewers can train themselves to notice 'red lights' in the answers – such as unusual terms, strong intonations and the like – which may signal a whole complex of topics important to the subject.

C. *Probing questions.* 'Could you say something more about that?'; 'Can you give a more detailed description of what happened?'; 'Do you have further examples of this?' The interviewer here pursues the answers, probing their content but without stating what dimensions are to be taken into account.

D. *Specifying questions.* The interviewer may also follow up with more operationalizing questions, for instance, 'What did you actually do when you felt a mounting anxiety?', 'How did your body react?' In an interview with many general statements, the interviewer can attempt to get more precise descriptions by asking 'Have you also experienced this yourself?'

E. *Direct questions.* The interviewer here directly introduces topics and dimensions, for example, 'Have you ever received money for good grades?', 'When you mention competition, do you then think of a sportsmanlike or a destructive competition?' Such direct questions may preferably be postponed until the later parts of the interview, after the subjects have given their own spontaneous descriptions and thereby indicated which aspects of the phenomenon are central to them.

F. *Indirect questions.* Here the interviewer may apply projective questions such as 'How do you believe other pupils regard the competition for grades?' The answer may refer directly to the attitudes of others; it may also be an indirect statement of the pupil's own attitude, which he or she does not state directly. Further careful questioning will be necessary here to interpret the answer.

G. *Structuring questions.* The interviewer is responsible for the course of the interview and should indicate when a theme has been exhausted. The interviewer may directly and politely break off long answers that are irrelevant to the investigation, for example by briefly stating his or her understanding of an answer, and then say 'I would now like to introduce another topic: … '

H. *Silence.* Rather than making the interview a cross-examination by continually firing off questions, the research interviewer can take a lead from therapists in employing silence to further the interview, following the adage 'silence is golden'. By allowing pauses in the conversation, the subjects have ample time to associate and reflect and then break the silence themselves with significant information.

(Continued)

(Continued)

l. *Interpreting questions.* The degree of interpretation may involve merely rephrasing an answer, for instance, 'You then mean that ... ?', or attempts at clarification: 'Is it correct that you feel that ... ?'; 'Does the expression ... cover what you have just expressed?' There may also be more direct interpretations of what the pupil has said: 'Is it correct that your main anxiety about the grades concerns the reaction from your parents?'

Box 5.2 depicts some main types of questions that may be useful, several of which were applied in the demonstration interview. The introductory question, asking about a specific episode of grading (SK 1/Question type A), hit home, and the first two-thirds of the interview were mainly a follow-up (B) of the student's answer (S 2) about the 'red star'. The term, and probably also her voice and facial expression, indicated that this was a symbol of some significant experience. My follow-up question, repeating 'red star' (SK 3/B), led to an emotional response rich in information (S 3).

Continued probing, repeating another significant expression – 'mixed emotions' – and probing for further description (SK 4/B and C) opened up to a basic conflict for the subject between loyalty to the teacher or to her peers. This theme was pursued until the concluding student remark, 'And what's more important to me is my friendships' (12). In some of the answers in this sequence I overheard potentially significant expressions like 'demarcation' and 'space' (S 5 and 8), and instead of following them up, posed specifying (SK 6/D) and interpreting (SK 9/I) questions.

The majority of questions in this interview were probing (C) – often by repeating significant words from the student's answers to the few direct questions about episodes and effects of grading. There were a few interpreting questions; early in the interview a direct interpretation of the student's statement (8) as 'Because of your good grades?' (SK 9/I) was immediately confirmed by a 'Yeah' (S 9). A later meaning-clarifying question, 'What do you mean by "rewarded"?' (SK 13/I) led to descriptions of specific rewards, such as getting ice-cream or staying up to watch TV (S 13).

There were also answers that I did not follow up, such as the student emphasizing 'What's more important to me is my friendships' (S 12). That is, I tried, by acknowledging what she said – 'That is the basic issue' (SK 13) – but when she did not pick it up, I changed the topic to reward for grades. I no longer know whether I chose not to pursue the friendship theme because I felt it was becoming too sensitive for her to elaborate further on in front of the class, or whether I sensed that she was changing my attempt to keep the interview within a discourse of grades to a discourse about friendships.

Box 5.3   Linguistic forms of questions

Can you describe it to me? What happened?
What did you do? How do you remember it? How did you experience it?
What do you feel about it? How was your emotional reaction to this event?
What do you think about it? How do you conceive of this issue?
What is your opinion of what happened? How do you judge it today?

The kind of knowledge produced in the interview depends to a considerable extent on the wording of the questions, which should be in line with the purpose of an interview study. In Box 5.3, different linguistic forms of a question asking for elaborating on an episode are suggested. The wording invites rather different styles of answers, ranging from descriptive, behavioural and experiential domains to emotional, cognitive and evaluative realms. A consistent use of one type of questioning throughout an interview may lead to a specific style of the answers, resulting in for example a predominantly emotional or conceptual interview.

The questions in the interview about grades (Box 5.1) were mostly matter-of-the fact questions, asking the student to 'remember' (SK 1 and 7), 'what happened' (SK 2 and 3) and to 'describe' (SK 4 and 5). There was a conceptual question 'what do you mean by' (SK 13). There were no direct questions about the feelings, but in two cases I repeated emotional terms the student used – 'mixed emotions' (SK 4) and 'feeling' (SK 8) – and the two questions asking for descriptions concerned the student's feelings of 'mixed emotions' and 'dissonance' (SK 4 and 5). In contrast, in the client-centred interview in Box 2.3, the counsellor predominantly used emotional terms in his questions, and Socrates applied inquisitive conceptual questions in his pursuit of the essence of love and beauty.

The art of second questions

Until now the focus has been on the interviewer's questions. Active listening – the interviewer's ability to listen actively to what the interviewee says – is as important as the specific mastery of questioning techniques. The interviewer needs to learn to listen to what is said and how it is said. We may note that in *Time Magazine's* biographies of the 20 most prominent scholars of the twentieth century (Chapter 1) it was the skills of Freud and Piaget to listen to and observe the patients and the children that were emphasized, in particular Freuds mastery of patient listening.

Decisions about which of the many dimensions of a subject's answer to pursue requires an ear for the theme and a knowledge of the interview topic, a sensitivity towards the social relationship of an interview, and the interviewer knowing what he or she wants to ask about. We may here perhaps draw an analogy with chess, where each move by the opponent changes the structure of the chessboard, and the player has to consider the multiple implications of the opponent's move before making his next move, anticipating the future moves of the opponent, and so on.

Box 5.4   Second questions

Pupil: Grades are often unjust, because very often – very often – they are only a measure of how much you talk, and how much you agree with the teacher's opinion.

Interviewer: How should that influence the grade?
Other potential interviewer responses:
  Silence …
  Hm, mm …
  'How much you talk'?

  Can you tell me more about that?
  Could you give some examples of what you are saying?
  Have you experienced this yourself?

  You feel that the grades are not fair?
  You find that the grades do not express your own abilities?

  Can you describe more grades as 'only a measure of how much you talk'?
  Could you specify how one follows the teacher's opinion?

  When you say grades depend upon how much you talk, do you then
    mean bluffing?
  When you mention importance of following teacher's opinion, are you
    thinking of wheedling?

  Are you sure that is correct?
  Is this not only your theory?

In Box 5.4 some potential interviewer responses are suggested to one interviewee statement about grades reported in Chapter 1. There is no one 'correct' follow-up question; the options suggested in the box open up to different aspects of the answer. The potential responses are grouped roughly, from merely indicating that the answer is heard and repeating a few words of the answer as an invitation to elaborate, to more specifically probing questions, and more or less interpreting questions, and finally some counter-questions are mentioned, the last one also being used by the interviewer in this case. The art of posing second questions can hardly be specified in advance, but requires a flexible on-the-spot follow-up of the subjects' answers, with consideration of the research questions of the interview inquiry.

Some of the ways in which I followed up the students' answers in the demonstration interview by asking for further descriptions, and clarification of meanings and of emotions, were discussed above. I experienced it as fairly easy to follow up on the student's answers as I was familiar with the topic and had conducted several interviews on grading in an investigation in Denmark (Box 4.3). I knew that in this short interview I wanted to demonstrate a specific interviewing technique to the class and show that this might bring interesting knowledge of a familiar topic, and I also hoped I might learn something about American students' relations to grading.

Key points

- A qualitative interview is usually semi-structured; it has a sequence of themes to be covered, as well as some prepared questions. Yet at the same time there is openness to changes of sequence and question forms in order to follow up the answers given and the stories told by the interviewees.
- The social interaction created in the interview situation is decisive for the readiness of the interviewee to answer the questions of importance to the interviewer, and for the quality of the answers.
- Careful attention should be given to setting the stage for an interview, with briefing of the subject before, and debriefing after, the interview. Consideration should be given to the effects of the briefing upon the knowledge produced in the interview and ethical implications for the interviewee.
- When preparing the script for an interview in the form of an interview guide, it may be useful to develop two lists of questions: one with the project's main research questions in academic language, and another with the research questions translated into the vernacular as questions to be posed during the interview.
- The quality of an interview relies not only on the questions posed; the way the interviewer reacts *after* an answer may be just as important, such as by allowing a pause for the interviewee to continue an answer, by probing for more information and by attempting to verify the answers given.

Further reading

Practical issues of conducting interviews are the topics of the following books:

Angrosino, M. (2007) *Doing Ethnographic and Observational Research*. (Book 3 of *The SAGE Qualitative Research Kit*). London: Sage.

Flick, U. (2007a) *Designing Qualitative Research* (Book 1 of *The SAGE Qualitative Research Kit*). London: Sage.

Rubin, H.J. and Rubin, I.S. (2005) *Qualitative Interviewing*. Thousand Oaks, CA: Sage.

Seidman, I.E. (1991) *Interviewing as Qualitative Research*. New York: Teachers College Press.

Spradley, J. (1979) *The Ethnographic Interview*. New York: Holt, Rinehart & Winston.

Wengraf, T. (2001) *Qualitative Research Interviewing*. Thousand Oaks, CA: Sage.

6
Interview variations

Interview subjects   67
Interview forms   70
Confrontational interviews   75

Chapter objectives
After reading this chapter, you should know

- some of the varieties of interviewing;
- some of the issues that may arise when interviewing different subjects, such as foreigners, children and elites;
- a heterogeneous range of interview forms, which are different tools
  among which the interviewer may choose, depending on the purpose of the inquiry, the kind of knowledge sought, the interview
  subjects, and the personal skills and style of the interviewer;
- that factual, conceptual and focus group interviews, as well as narrative and discursive interviews, each imply different social dynamics and questioning techniques; and
- the contrast between the more harmonic empathetic life-world
  interviews of the preceding chapter and more agonistic confrontational forms of interviewing.

Interview subjects

The interview form discussed in the preceding chapter pertained to middle-class
adult subjects in Northern Europe and America. Different issues pertain to interviewing children and elites, for interviewing men and women, for police suspects
and witnesses, and for interviewing across cultures. In particular, foreign cultures
may involve different norms for interactions with strangers concerning initiative,
directness, modes of questioning and the like. I shall highlight some of the

issues raised by interviewing different populations by focusing on cross-cultural interviews and interviews with children and elites.

Interviewing subjects across cultures

With cross-cultural interviewing it is difficult to become aware of the multitude of cultural factors that affect the relationship between interviewer and interviewee. In a foreign culture an interviewer needs time to establish a familiarity with the new culture and learn some of the many verbal and non-verbal factors where interviewers in a foreign culture may go amiss. For example, the simple word 'yes' is in some cultures heard as an agreement, whereas in other cultures it is a response just confirming that the question has been heard, a difference that may be crucial in, for instance, negotiations of business contracts. Extra-linguistic features of communication may also give rise to intercultural misunderstanding such as when cultural groups use similar gestures, but with different meanings intended; thus nodding, which in most parts of Europe signifies agreement, in several areas of Greece means no (Ryen, 2002).

Some of the specific factors that may be critical in cross-cultural interviewing include asking questions as a means of obtaining information; making direct rather than circuitous replies; referring directly to matters that are taboo; looking into a person's face when speaking; sending a man to interview a woman, and vice versa (Keats, 2000). In addition to this, the linguistic and social issues of translation are important. Care should be taken to select an interpreter who is culturally acceptable as well as proficient in the language. The role of the interpreter is to assist, and not to take over the role of the interviewer or the interviewee. In particular, this may be a risk when, instead of using an official translator, a relative or friend serves as an interpreter. While this may facilitate contact, the familiar interpreter may have an agenda of his or her own and subtly enter into an interviewer or interviewee role.

Difficulties in recognizing disparities in language use, gestures and cultural norms may also arise when interviewing across gender and generation, social class and religion, within a researcher's own culture. Such differences between subcultures may not be as pronounced as between different cultures, but with an implicit assumption of existing in a common culture, intra-cultural variations may be difficult to detect.

Interviews with children

Interviews with children allow them to give voice to their own experiences and understanding of their world. In particular, Piaget's interviews with children about their physical concepts and understanding of reality and morality have shaped our current views of children's thought processes.

Box 6.1   Piaget's interview about a child's dreams

Piaget:	Where does the dream come from?
Child (5 years):	I think you sleep so well that you dream.
Piaget:	Does it come from us or from outside?
Child:	From outside.
Piaget:	What do we dream with?
Child:	I don't know.
Piaget:	With the hands? ... With nothing?
Child:	Yes, with nothing.
Piaget:	When you are in bed and you dream, where is the dream?
Child:	In my bed, under the blanket. I don't really know. If it was in my stomach, the bones would be in the way and I shouldn't see it.
Piaget:	Is the dream there when you sleep?
Child:	Yes, it is in the bed beside me.

Source: Piaget (1930, pp. 97–8).

In the interview passage in Box 6.1, Piaget consistently challenges the child's understanding of the location of dreams, thereby attempting to arrive at the child's conception of dreams. However, we may note that in this passage it is the adult interviewer who introduces and persists with questions about the spatial location of dreams, a dimension that does not seem to be a central issue for the child. The child appears to be influenced by the interviewer's suggestions, thus twice repeating verbatim the interviewer's proposals as his own answers: 'from outside' and 'with nothing'.

The influence of leading questions becomes crucial in criminal cases. The reliability of information obtained through interviews with children is critical in court cases about child abuse. Children may be reluctant to talk to a stranger about painful events. Children are also easily led by the questions of adults and may provide unreliable or directly false information.

While it may be a truism that children and adults live in different social worlds, the many differences may be easy to overlook when interviewing children. Some barriers between children and adults may be bridged when interviewing children in natural settings. Eder and Fingerson (2002) draw attention to the power imbalance between the child and the adult, and the need to avoid the interviewer being associated with the classroom teacher as well as to refrain from conveying expectations that there is one right answer to a question. It is important to use age-appropriate questions, and some difficulties of interviews with adults may be aggravated in interviews with children, such as the interviewer asking long and complex questions and posing more than one question at a time. In quite a few instances, interviews with children may preferably take place within the context of some other task, such as drawing, reading a story, watching cartoons and videos, or playing with dolls and cars. Many of Piaget's interviews were carried out in relation to experimental tasks, such as the child judging the weight or size of objects.

Interviews with elites

Elite interviews are with persons who are leaders or experts in a community, people who are usually in powerful positions. Obtaining access to the interviewees is a key problem when studying elites, as discussed by Hertz and Imber (1995) in their anthology on elite interviews. When an interview is established, the prevailing power asymmetry of the interview situation may be cancelled out by the powerful position of the elite interviewee.

Elites are used to being asked about their opinions and thoughts, and an interviewer with some expertise in the interview topic may provide an interesting conversation partner. The interviewer should be knowledgeable about the topic of concern and master the technical language, as well as being familiar with the social situation and biography of the interviewee. An interviewer demonstrating that he or she has a sound knowledge of the interview topic will gain respect and be able to achieve an extent of symmetry in the interview relationship. Experts may be used to being interviewed, and may more or less have prepared 'talk tracks' to promote the viewpoints they want to communicate by means of the interview, which requires considerable skill from the interviewer to get beyond. Elite interviewees will tend to have a secure status, where it may be feasible to challenge their statements, with the provocations possibly leading to new insights. Interviews with experts, where the interviewer confronts and also contributes with his or her conceptions of the interview theme, may approximate the intense questioning of a Socratic dialogue.

Interview forms

A variety of research interview forms, useful for different purposes, exist. Whereas factual and conceptual interviews are in accord with a miner metaphor of interviewing, in seeking facts and concepts that are there already, discursive and most forms of narrative interviews are in line with a traveller metaphor of the interviewer and the interviewees co-constructing knowledge through the discourses and narratives. With the broad variety of interview forms and subjects described in this chapter it becomes understandable that there are no general standard procedures and rules for research interviewing. The specific recommendations for conducting a semi-structured life-world interview in Chapter 5 have different relevance for the variety of forms and subjects of interview described in the present chapter.

Factual interviews

Qualitative interviews do not only focus on the interviewees' own perspectives and meanings. Obtaining valid factual information may be crucial in many interviews. Thus, in professional settings it may be vital for a medical doctor interviewing a child, or its parents, to acquire correct information about the exact bottle of medical pills the child had eaten from. In forensic interviews it can be imperative for a police officer or lawyer to gain valid information about whether the accused had a knife in his hand or not. Interviewing about a suspect's intentions with a knife involves a different kind of questioning. In less dramatic settings, when interviewing for the oral history of a community, the focus will be less on the storyteller's own perspective upon the events recounted, than on his or her stories as venues to reliable information about a collective past.

The intricacies of interviewing for factual information are well documented by studies in witness psychology. The importance of the wording of questions was forcefully brought out in an experiment where different groups of subjects were shown the same film of two cars colliding and afterwards asked about the cars' speed. The average speed estimate in reply to the question 'About how fast were the cars going when they contacted each other?' was 32 mph. Other subjects – seeing the same film, but with '*contacted*' replaced by '*smashed*' in the question – gave an average speed estimate of 41 mph (Loftus and Palmer, 1974). Such experiments may serve interviewers as a reminder to be extremely careful in wording their questions when interviewing for factual information.

Conceptual interviews

The purpose of an interview may be a conceptual clarification. An interviewer may here want to chart the conceptual structure of a subject's, or a group of subjects', conceptions of phenomena such as 'fairness' and 'competition', 'respect' and 'responsibility' (the latter concept is explored in a confrontational interview shown in Box 6.3) The questions will explore the meaning and the conceptual dimensions of these terms, as well as their positions and links within a conceptual network. The intricacies of interviewing for conceptual networks are manifested in anthropologists' studies of kinship structures in a foreign culture, where the questioning may concern finding the linguistic terms for the different types of relatives, and establish whether, for example, there are different terms for elder and younger, female and male, or second cousins, as well as whether the terms depend on the gender of the person speaking. A conceptual interview may also be in the form of a joint endeavour to uncover the essential nature of a phenomenon, such as in Socrates and Agathon's inquiry to establish the essence of beauty.

Focus group interviews

While academic interviews have generally been one-to-one interviews, there is today an increasing use of focus group interviews. Social researchers had employed group interviews in the 1920s, whereas a widespread use of group interviewing first took place after the 1950s, when market researchers developed what they termed the focus group interview to investigate consumer motives and product preferences. Today focus groups dominate consumer research, ranging from the promotion of cereals to the marketing of politicians. They are also being applied in a variety of fields such as health education and in evaluation of social programs, and since the 1980s they have entered academic social research (see Barbour, 2007).

A focus group usually consists of six to ten subjects led by a moderator (Chrzanowska, 2002). The focus groups are characterized by a non-directive style of interviewing, where the prime concern is to encourage a variety of viewpoints on the topic in focus for the group. The group moderator introduces the topics for discussion and facilitates the discussion. The moderator's task is to create a permissive atmosphere for the expression of personal and conflicting viewpoints on the topics in focus. As mentioned earlier, this form of interviewing requires extensive training; according to Chrzanowska, several years' practice is required to become a proficient focus group moderator.

The aim of the focus group is not to reach consensus about, or solutions to, the issues discussed, but to bring forth different viewpoints on an issue. Focus group interviews are well suited for exploratory studies in a new domain since the lively collective interaction may bring forth more spontaneous expressive and emotional views than in individual, often more cognitive interviews. In the case of sensitive taboo topics, the group interaction may facilitate expression of viewpoints usually not accessible. The group interaction reduces the moderator's control of the course of an interview, and one price of the lively interaction may be interview transcripts that are somewhat chaotic.

Narrative interviews

Narrative interviews focus on the stories the subjects tell, on the plots and structures of their accounts. The stories may come up spontaneously during the interview or be elicited by the interviewer. In a study on narratives in interview research, *Research Interviewing – Context and Narrative* (1986), Mishler outlined how interviews understood as narratives emphasize the temporal, the social and the meaning structures of the interview. In everyday conversations, answers to questions often display the features of narratives, and Mishler posits that when stories appear so often, it supports the view that narratives are one of the natural cognitive and linguistic forms through which individuals attempt to organize and express meaning.

Box 6.2   A craftsman's narrative

I: And uh I'd like to start by asking you uh about the beginning/ uh how you u:uh got into the . work that you now do. What was hapening then? a:ah What led you into it?

R: hm hmm … hh well it's- it's strange

It ah- it ah- When I first started ah doing woodworking
I got into a program in- in a- a trade school/ in high school level
and (sigh) it kin- I was from a working class background
so.hh the options seemed to be pretty limited to me.

But I always had an interest in building
even when I was in grammar school.
I was always building at night you=know
like making airplane models and things like that.
Those were the things tha- I-
Then I got to a point where I began to get experimental
and more interested in uh doing things on my own
so I would sort of design the airplane/ and build it you=know/ and
    see if I could make it fly
that kind of thing.

But then- and so my- to continue my interests/ I got into the wood-
    working program in the- in the-in the trade school
and it- I got bored stiff you=know.

Just- uh they- they took patterns down off the walls/and you=know
    it- uh build tha- that kind of thing.
I wasn't very interested in rebuilding like reproductions and things
    like that
so … hh I- I quit that.

Source: Mishler (1999, pp. 73–4).

Box 6.2 depicts the start of a narrative interview with a furniture craftsman-artist by Mishler. The initial question about how the craftsman got into his work opened up to a spontaneous story about the demotivating effect trade school had on him. On the form side we may note how Mishler has chosen to render the transcript verbatim and in a style close to a poem, where the poetic shape provides an accessible structure of the story. He also includes annotations, which keep the transcription close to the original oral style, but which may be distracting to an inexperienced reader (some of the annotations for the transcription are explained in Box 8.1).

In a narrative interview the interviewer can ask directly for stories and perhaps together with the interviewee attempt to structure the different happenings recounted into coherent stories. The interviewer may introduce the interview with a question about specific episodes such as 'Can you please tell me the story of what happened at the demonstration when the police broke it up?', or for an institutional period 'Can you tell me about how you came to the hospital and what happened during your stay there?', or ask for a life story: 'Please tell me about your life – you were born in … at …?' After the initial request for a story, the main role of the interviewer is to remain a listener, abstaining from interruptions, occasionally posing questions for clarification, and assisting the interviewee in continuing to tell his story. Through his questions, nods and silences the interviewer is a co-producer of the narrative. When spontaneous stories appear during a common semi-structured interview, the interviewer can encourage the subjects to let their stories unfold, and also assist the subjects to structure their stories. Being familiar with narrative structures, the interviewer may take care to unfold temporal sequences, focus on who is the hero of the story, who are the antagonists and who the protagonists of the hero, try to ascertain what is the main plot of the story, the possible subplots, and elements of tensions, conflicts and resolutions.

Narrative interviews may serve multiple purposes, of which three will be pointed out. First, a narrative can refer to a specific episode or course of action significant to the narrator, leading to a *short story*. Second, the narrative may concern the interviewee's life story as seen through the actor's own perspective, and is then called a *life history,* or biographical interview (Rosenthal, 2004). Third, there is the *oral history* interview, where the topic goes beyond the individual's history to cover communal history; here the interviewee is an informant for recording the oral history of a community (Bornat, 2004; Yow, 1994).

Discursive interviews

Discourse analysis focuses on how knowledge and truth is created within discourses, and on the power relations of discourses (see Rapley, 2007). All interviews appear as discourses; interviewers working within a discursive framework will, however, be particularly attentive to specific aspects of the interaction of the interview discourse, which differ from conventional interviewing: 'First, variation in response is as important as consistency. Second, techniques, which allow diversity rather than those which eliminate it are emphasized, resulting in more informal conversational exchanges and third, interviewers are seen as active participants rather than like speaking questionnaires' (Potter and Wetherell, 1987, p. 165).

A discursive perspective sensitizes the interviewer to differences in the discourses of the researcher and the subjects during an interview, and their differential power to define the discourses. A discursive interviewer will be attentive to and, in some cases, stimulate confrontations between the different discourses in play. During the grade interview presented in the previous chapter, I was not aware of how the student attempted to turn my intended discourse on grades into a discourse about friendships. Another example of diverging discourses of researcher and interviewee will be given by an interview on crossing discourses (Box 7.4; see also Rapley, 2007).

Confrontational interviews

Active interviewing contrasts with the prevailing forms of empathetic and consensus-seeking interviewing. Holstein and Gubrium (1995) have argued for active interviews, where the interviewer activates narrative production, suggesting narrative positions, resources and orientations. Provoked by the interactional and informational challenges of the interview situation, the respondent becomes a kind of researcher in his or her own right, actively composing meaning by way of situated, assisted inquiry, where the interaction between interviewer and respondent is a reality-constructing process.

A direct confrontational approach brings the conflict and power dimensions of the interview conversation. Such an agonistic understanding of the conversation is at the root of Lyotard's analysis of knowledge in the postmodern society. He regards every statement as a move in a game, which is 'at the base of our entire method: namely that to speak is to fight, in the meaning of a game, and that speech acts go forth from a general agonistics' (1984, p. xx). Agonistic interviewing enhances confrontation, where the interviewer deliberately provokes conflicts and divergences of interests, as seen in some forms of journalistic interviews. In contrast to an ideal of consensus and harmony, the interview becomes a battleground where the interviewer contradicts and challenges the interviewee's statements, whereby conflicts and power become visible. The position of the interviewer comes more into the open in a confrontational interview, with options for the subject to challenge the interviewer's assumptions, approximating a more equal power balance of the interview interaction. The goal of the confrontational interview is to lead to insight through dialectical development of opposites, such as in Socrates' dialectical and agonistic questioning of the Sophists.

Bellah and co-workers were inspired by the Socratic dialogue in their interviews about North American values. In contrast to regarding the interviewer as a friend, or therapist, probing deeply into the private psyche of the interviewee, Bellah and co-workers practised what they call *active interviews*, which 'create the possibility of *public* conversation and argument' (Bellah et al., 1985, p. 305; original emphasis). Active interviews do not necessarily aim for agreement between interviewer and subject, and the researcher may challenge what the interviewee says.

Box 6.3 An active challenging interview

Q: So what are you responsible for?
A: I'm responsible for my acts and for what I do.
Q: Does that mean you're responsible for others, too?
A: No.
Q: Are you your sister's keeper?
A: No.
Q: Your brother's keeper?
A: No.
 (...)
Q: What about children?
A: I ... I would say I have a legal responsibility for them, but in a sense I think they in turn are responsible for their own acts.

Source: Bellah et al. (1985, p. 304).

In the interview sequence in Box 6.3 the interviewer tries to discover at what point the subject would take responsibility for another human being. After a series of questions it is only when asked about responsibility for her own children that the respondent's initial claim that she is only responsible for her own acts is challenged. The Socratic stance in the interview is described in this way: 'Though we did not seek to impose our ideas on those with whom we talked, ... we did attempt to uncover assumptions, to make explicit what the person we were talking to might have left implicit' (Bellah et al., 1985, p. 304).

Bourdieu et al. likewise confronted the subjects in their study of social suffering among the downtrodden in France. In the interview sequence in Box 1.3, his compassion for the plight of the young men did not prevent him from posing inquisitive questions and proposing conflicting interpretations of their accounts. This included direct questions such as 'You are not telling the whole story', and leading questions to information suspected withheld: 'What were you doing, bugging him?'. In an outline of his interview approach 'Understanding' in an appendix to *The Weight of the World*, Bourdieu also compares his interviewing to Socrates' questioning: 'The "Socratic" work of aiding explanations aims to propose and not to impose. To formulate suggestions sometimes explicitly presented as such ("you don't mean that ... ") and intended to offer multiple, open-ended continuations to the interviewee's argument, to their hesitations or searching for appropriate expression' (Bourdieu et al., 1999, pp. 614–15).

The utilization of confrontational interview forms depends upon the subjects interviewed; to some subjects strong challenges to their basic belief may be an ethical transgression, while confident respondents, such as elite interviewees, may be stimulated by the intellectual challenges. A confrontational interview may thus approximate a mutual and egalitarian relationship where both parties pose questions and give answers, with a reciprocal criticism of what the other says. The research interview may then become a conversation, which stimulates intervie-wee and interviewer to formulate their ideas about the research topics, to learn and to increase their knowledge of the subject matter of inquiry.

Key points

- There is no correct or ideal interview form; the appropriate mode of interviewing depends on the topic and purpose of the interview, on the interview subjects and the epistemological conceptions of knowledge sought.
- Different interview subjects entail different social relations and styles of questioning, such as when interviewing members of a foreign culture, or children and elites in the researcher's own culture.
- Interviews seeking distinct types of knowledge for specific purposes will take different forms. Interviews seeking witness reports of what hap-pened in a specific situation, interviews describing spontaneous experi-ences, interviews seeking personal narratives and interviews aiming to uncover implicit cognitive assumptions involve different rules of the game.
- In addition to a prevalent empathetic and consensual interview form, the more active confrontational and agonistic styles of interviewing may also produce valuable knowledge.

Further reading

The differences between group and single interviews are spelled out in the follow-ing books in more detail:

Barbour, R. (2007) *Doing Focus Groups* (Book 4 of *The SAGE Qualitative Research Kit*). London: Sage.
Chrzanowska, J. (2002) *Interviewing Groups and Individuals in Qualitative Market Research*. Thousand Oaks, CA: Sage.
Gubrium, J.F. and Holstein, J.A. (eds) (2002) *Handbook of Interview Research*. Thousand Oaks, CA: Sage.
Hertz, R. and Imber, J.B. (eds) (1995) *Studying Elites Using Qualitative Methods*. Thousand Oaks, CA: Sage.
Memon, A. and Bull, R. (eds) (2000) *Handbook of the Psychology of Interviewing*. New York: Wiley.

7
Interview quality

Hamlet's interview   78
Interview quality   80
Interviewer qualifications   81
Standard objections to the quality of interview research   84
Leading questions   88
Tensions of scientific and ethical responsibility   89

Chapter objectives
After reading this chapter, you should know

- quality criteria for good interviewing practice;
- from the example from *Hamlet*, how judgement of the quality of an interview depends its purpose and content;
- quality criteria for a good, and for an ideal, interview;
- standards for the craftsmanship of interviewing in the semi-structured life world interview described in Chapter 5;
- that the varieties of interviewing discussed in Chapter 6 may involve different quality criteria;
- epistemological issues pertaining to the quality of interview-produced knowledge in relation to some standard external objections to interview quality and for the example of leading questions; and
- how methodological and ethical criteria of good interviewing may in some cases be at odds with each other.

Hamlet's interview

A dramatic case (Box 7.1) may exemplify how the appraisal of an interview technique depends on the content and the purpose of the interview.

Box 7.1   Hamlet's interview

Hamlet: Do you see yonder cloud that's almost in shape of a camel?
Polonius: By th' mass, and 'tis like a camel indeed.
Hamlet: Methinks it is like a weasel.
Polonius: It is back'd like a weasel.
Hamlet: Or like a whale?
Polonius: Very like a whale.
Hamlet: (Aside) They fool me to the top of my bent.

(*Hamlet*, act III, scene 2)

A first comment on the quality of this interview concerns its length. Hamlet's interview is brief. The seven lines are, however, dense and rich enough to instigate more lengthy comments. In contrast, current research interviews are often too long and filled with idle chatter. If one knows what to ask for, why one is asking, and how to ask, one can conduct short interviews that are rich in meaning.

The quality of Hamlet's interview technique depends on how the purpose of the interview is understood. This short passage gives rise to several interpretations. At first glance the interview is an example of an unreliable technique – by using three leading questions, Hamlet leads Polonius to give three entirely different answers. Thus the interview does not yield any reproducible, reliable knowledge about the *shape of the cloud* in question.

At second glance, the topic of the interview might change: the figure in question is no longer the cloud, but the *personality of Polonius* and his trustworthiness. The interview then provides reliable, thrice-checked knowledge about Polonius as an unreliable person – his three different answers are all led by Hamlet's questions. With the change in the purpose and the topic of the interview the leading questions do not produce entirely unreliable knowledge, but involve an indirect, reliable, interview technique.

Hamlet's interview then approximates a threefold ideal of being interpreted, validated and reported at the end of the interview. By repeating the question in different versions and each time getting the 'same' indirect answer about Polonius's trustworthiness, the inter-view is 'self-interpreted' before Hamlet closes off with his aside interpretation: 'They fool me to the top of my bent.' As to the second requirement – verification – few interview researchers today repeat so consistently as Hamlet a question in different versions to test the reliability of their subject's answers. Regarding the third requirement – reporting – the short interview has been carried out so well that it speaks for itself. I would believe that, when watching the play, the audience would generally experience a gestalt switch from the shape of the cloud to the trustworthiness of Polonius as the interview topic, even before Hamlet gives his aside conclusion.

So far, I have discussed Hamlet's interview isolated from the context of the broader drama. At third glance the interview appears as a display of the *power relations* at a royal court. The prince displays his power to make a courtier say anything he wants. Or, the courtier shows his mode of managing the power relations at the court. In an earlier scene in the play, Polonius had demonstrated his mastery of interview technique in a lesson on 'by indirections to find directions out'. When Polonius is that well versed in questioning techniques, is he actually caught by Hamlet's questions? Or does he see through the scheme and play up to Hamlet as expected of a courtier?

From an ethical perspective, the evaluation of Hamlet's interview also depends on the interpretation of its purpose and content. In the first reading, the leading questions merely lead to unreliable knowledge of the shape of the cloud. In the second reading, the interview entails the deliberate deception of Polonius; there is no question of informed consent, and the consequences may be a matter of life and death for the protagonists of the drama. Here an ethics of principles is overruled by a utilitarian interest in survival.

The quality and the ethicality of Hamlet's interview are dependent on the interpretation of the content and the purpose of this specific interview. With the different topics and objectives of interviews, and the variety of forms, in mind, I shall nevertheless suggest some criteria for evaluating the quality of a research interview and the craftsmanship of the interviewer.

Interview quality

The quality of the original interviews is decisive for the quality of the subsequent analysis, verification and reporting of the interview findings. A sophisticated theoretical analysis based upon interviews of dubious quality may turn out to be a magnificent edifice built on sand.

Box 7.2   Quality criteria for an interview

- The extent of spontaneous, rich, specific and relevant answers from the interviewee.
- The shorter the interviewer's questions and the longer the subjects' answers, the better.
- The degree to which the interviewer follows up and clarifies the meanings of the relevant aspects of the answers.
- To a large extent the interview is interpreted throughout the interview.
- The interviewer attempts to verify his or her interpretations of the subject's answers in the course of the interview.
- The interview is 'self-reported', it is a self-reliant story that hardly requires extra explanations.

Of the six quality criteria for a semi-structured interview proposed in Box 7.2, the last three, in particular, refer to an ideal interview – suggesting that the meaning of what is said is interpreted, verified and reported by the time the tape recorder is turned off. This demands craftsmanship and expertise and presupposes that the interviewer knows what he or she is interviewing about, as well as why and how. Although such quality criteria might seem to be unattainable ideals, they can serve as guidelines for good interview practice. The examples given in this book of the interviews by Socrates and Hamlet do fulfil such ideal criteria; they provide a coherent unity in themselves and present rich texts for further interpretations (see also Flick, 2007b).

Interviewer qualifications

The interviewer is the key research instrument of an interview inquiry. A good interviewer knows the topic of the interview, masters conversational skills and is proficient in language, with an ear for his or her subjects' linguistic style. The interviewer must continually make on-the-spot decisions about what to ask and how; which aspects of a subject's answer to follow up, and which not; which answers to comment and interpret, and which not. The interviewer should have a sense for good stories and be able to assist the subjects in the unfolding of their narratives.

Box 7.3   Interviewer qualifications

Knowledgeable: Has an extensive knowledge of the interview theme and can conduct an informed conversation about the topic; will know what issues are important to pursue, without attempting to shine with his or her extensive knowledge.

Structuring: Introduces a purpose for the interview, outlines the procedure in passing and rounds off the interview by, for example, briefly telling what was learned in the course of the conversation and asking whether the interviewee has any questions concerning the situation.

Clear: Poses clear, simple, easy and short questions; speaks distinctly and understandably, does not use academic language or professional jargon. The exception is in a stress interview; then the questions can be complex and ambiguous, with the subjects' answers revealing their reactions to stress.

(Continued)

(Continued)

Gentle: Allows subjects to finish what they are saying, lets them proceed at their own rate of thinking and speaking. Is easy-going, tolerates pauses, indicates that it is acceptable to put forward unconventional and provocative opinions and to treat emotional issues.

Sensitive: Listens actively to the content of what is said, hears the many nuances of meaning in an answer and seeks to get the nuances of meaning described more fully. The interviewer is empathetic, listens to the emotional message in what is said, not only hearing what is said but also how it is said, and notices as well what is not said. The interviewer feels when a topic is too emotional to pursue in the interview.

Open: Hears which aspects of the interview topic are important for the interviewee. Listens with an evenly hovering attention, is open to new aspects that can be introduced by the interviewee, and follows them up.

Steering: Knows what he or she wants to find out: is familiar with the purpose of the interview, what it is important to acquire knowledge about. The interviewer controls the course of the interview and is not afraid of interrupting digressions from the interviewee.

Critical: Does not take everything that is said at face value, but questions critically to test the reliability and validity of what the interviewees tell. This critical checking can pertain to the observational evidence of the interviewees' statements as well as to their logical consistency.

Remembering: Retains what a subject has said during the interview, can recall earlier statements and ask to have them elaborated, and can relate what has been said during different parts of the interview to each other.

Interpreting: Manages throughout the interview to clarify and extend the meanings of the interviewee's statements; provides interpretations of what is said, which may then be confirmed or disconfirmed by the interviewee.

Interviewer qualifications, such as those outlined in Box 7.3, may lead to good interviews in the sense of producing rich knowledge and ethically creating a beneficial situation for the subjects. The qualifications summed up here may differ for various types of interviews, and in interviews in which the topic really matters, the technical rules and criteria may lose relevance when confronted with the existential importance of the interview topic. With extensive practice in different interview forms and with different subjects, an experienced interviewer might go beyond technical recommendations and criteria, and – sometimes – deliberately disregard or break the rules. Also interviews by less experienced interviewers, which do not fulfil common interview guidelines, may in some cases provide worthwhile information.

Box 7.4 Crossing interview discourses

Interviewer: One thing I have been wondering. A lot of you guys stay after work to do troubleshooting on your own equipment or moonlighting?

Pupil: Yes.

Interviewer: What do you learn from that?

Pupil: It depends on what kind of moonlighting we do. Of course it is just routine, our interest to be allowed to potter around with something in which we see some benefit. If you have an old computer monitor at home and its broken then you bring it and fiddle with it to see if you can find the trouble. It's not ... you know, we are not allowed to potter with our television at work. You do not learn that, you learn about an instrument. To build your own amplifier is also something else than measuring some electronic equipment down here.

Interviewer: Okay, so you do it to get some experience with more types of instruments and equipment?

Pupil: No, it's not to become experienced, it's done to apply what you have learned at school for your own profit. Such a computer monitor – you get a new one without having to buy one. If you build an amplifier, well, then you might, it's much cheaper than having to buy one yourself. It's not to learn something extra; it's done simply out of simple interest. Or because there is some cool cash involved in repairing the video of a friend.

...

Interviewer: Okay. You express sort of a contradiction when you say it's not to learn something, it's just your interest?

Pupil: You don't think of it as learning.

Interviewer: But you learn something through it?

(Continued)

(Continued)

Pupil: Yes, but it's not like when you come home from school and say, I don't understand this, now I want to learn it. And then you go and ask for a task where it's involved. It's not like you go and choose a monitor to learn about it. You have a monitor at home, which is broken and you decide to fix it. Then you find out something about it.

Source: Tanggaard (2007, pp. 169–70).

In the crossing discourses of Box 7.4 the interviewer is clearly not sensitive to what a vocational pupil tries to tell her about his work. The researcher and the pupil talk in crossing discourses regarding which of his activities were to be considered as learning. In contrast to many interviewees, he is not subjected to the power position of the researcher, but takes a strong position against the researcher about whether his activities constitute learning or not. The researcher was investigating the learning of electronics at a vocational school and she had obvious problems in getting this pupil to talk about learning – the very topic of her PhD project. During the interview she was not aware of how she and the pupil were following crossing discourses about what constituted learning – discourses that hardly touched each other. When analyzing the interview transcript later, after having read Foucault on discourse analysis, she came to regard this sequence, and also her interviews with other pupils, as 'discourses crossing swords', yielding important information about which activities the pupil considered as learning and which not.

The issue of interview quality goes beyond the craftsmanship of the individual interviewer and raises epistemological and ethical issues of pursuing interview knowledge. I shall now first turn from quality criteria, internal to interview research, to some common external criticisms of the quality of interview-produced knowledge.

Standard objections to the quality of interview research

Box 7.5 Standard criticisms of qualitative interviews

The qualitative research interview is *not*:

1. scientific, but only reflects common sense
2. quantitative, but only qualitative
3. objective, but subjective
4. scientific hypothesis testing, but only exploratory

(Continued)

(Continued)

5. a scientific method, since it is too person-dependent
6. trustworthy, but biased
7. reliable, since it rests upon leading questions
8. intersubjective, since different readers find different meanings
9. valid, as it relies on subjective impressions
10. generalizable, because there are too few subjects

Interview reports have tended to evoke rather standardized objections about their quality from the mainstream of modern social science. In Box 7.5, ten typical criticisms of interview research are listed; the first four refer to general conceptions of scientific research, the next three to the interviewing and analysis stages, and the last two to validation and generalization. Some of the objections refer to intrinsic problems of interview research, whereas others arise from an inadequate understanding of the use of conversations as a research method. Below I give some rhetorical suggestions for responding to such standard objections, summarizing points made earlier and anticipating arguments in the coming chapters. This overview may save novice interview researchers some of the time and energy often used for external defence, to the benefit of more intensive internal work with interview quality. If an objection is considered valid to the specific interview investigation, it can be taken into account when designing the study and thereby improve the quality of the research. If an objection is regarded as invalid, the arguments for this can be presented in the report.

1. The qualitative research interview is not scientific, but only reflects common sense

No single authoritative definition of science exists, according to which the interview can be unequivocally categorized as scientific or unscientific. A working definition of science may be suggested as the methodical production of new, systematic knowledge. The question of scientific or not then depends on the understanding of the key terms in this definition, such as *methodical, new, systematic* and *knowledge*, in relation to the specific interview investigation.

2. Interviews are not quantitative, only qualitative, and thus not scientific

In paradigmatic social science discussions, science has often been equated with quantification. In the research practice of the natural and the social sciences, however, qualitative analysis also has a major position. To take a simple example: at the time of finishing this book (January 2006), a Google search on 'qualitative analysis chemistry' yielded more than 2 million hits and 'qualitative analysis social science' 11 million hits (with 'quantitative' in the search, the concerned hits were over 7 million and 17 million, respectively). In mainstream social science textbooks on method, however, the qualitative aspects of the research process have hardly existed until recently.

3. The qualitative research interview is not objective, but subjective

The basic terms of this objection are ambiguous. The objectivity and subjectivity of interview research needs to be discussed specifically for each of the multiple meanings of objectivity and subjectivity relevant to the interview inquiry in question (Chapter 10).

4. Qualitative interviews do not test hypotheses; they are only exploratory and thus not scientific

In a broad conception of science as hypothesis testing, as well as descriptive and exploratory, designs are important, with description and exploration as strong points of qualitative research. And, contrary to the objection, an interview may also take the form of a process of continual hypothesis testing, where the interviewer tests hypotheses, with the interplay of direct questions, counter-questions, leading questions and probing questions.

5. The interview is not a scientific method, it is too person-dependent

A research interview is flexible, context-sensitive and dependent on the personal interrelationship of the interviewer and interviewee. Rather than attempt to eliminate the influence of the personal interaction of interviewer and interviewee, we might regard the person of the interviewer as the primary research instrument for obtaining knowledge, which puts strong demands on the quality of his or her knowledge, their empathy and their craftsmanship.

6. Interview results are not trustworthy; they are biased

The answer needs to be concrete – the specific counter-question concerns who cannot be trusted and in what sense. Unacknowledged bias may entirely invalidate the results of an interview inquiry. A recognized bias or subjective perspective may, however, come to highlight specific aspects of the phenomenon being investigated and bring new dimensions forward, contributing to a multi-perspectival construction of knowledge.

7. Might not the interview results be due to leading questions, and thus unreliable?

The leading effects of leading questions are well documented. The qualitative interview is, however, also well suited to systematically applying leading questions to check the reliability of the interviewees' answers, to be exemplified in the following section.

8. The interpretation of interviews is not intersubjective, but subjective, as different readers find different meanings

We may here distinguish between an unacknowledged biased subjectivity, to be avoided, and a perspectival subjectivity. With a clarification of the perspectives adopted towards an interview text, several interpretations of the same text need not be a weakness, but a strong point of interview research.

9. Interviewing is not a valid method, it depends on subjective impressions

Interviewing is a personal craft, the quality of which depends on the craftsmanship of the researcher. Here validation becomes a matter of the researcher's ability to continually check, question and theoretically interpret the findings.

10. Interview findings are not generalizable; there are too few subjects

The number of subjects necessary depends on the purpose of the study. In postmodern conceptions of social sciences the goal of global generalization is replaced by a transferability of knowledge from one situation to another, taking into account the contextuality and heterogeneity of social knowledge.

In a reinterpretation, the standard objections can be reversed and read as pointing to the strong points of qualitative interview research. The force of the interview is its privileged access to the subjects' everyday world. The deliberate use of the subjective perspective need not be a negative bias; rather, the personal perspectives of interviewees and interviewer can provide a distinctive and sensitive understanding of the everyday life world. A controlled use of leading questions may lead to well-controlled knowledge. A plurality of interpretations enriches the meanings of the everyday world, and the person of the researcher is the most sensitive instrument available to investigate human meanings. The explorative potentialities of the interview can open to qualitative descriptions of new phenomena. Validating and generalizing from interview findings open up alternative modes of evaluating the quality and objectivity of qualitative research.

Leading questions

The question most likely to be asked about interview quality concerns leading questions, sometimes raised in the form of a question such as 'Cannot the interview results be due to leading questions?' The very form of the question involves a liar's paradox: an answer of 'Yes, this is a serious danger' may be due to the suggestive formulation of the question leading to this answer. And a 'No, this is not the case' may demonstrate that leading questions are not that powerful.

It is a well-documented finding that even a slight rewording of a question in a questionnaire or in the interrogation of eyewitnesses may influence the answer. When the results of public opinion polls are published, the proponents of a political party receiving low support are usually quick to find biases in the wording of the poll's questions. Politicians are well experienced in warding off leading questions from reporters; but if leading questions are inadvertently posed to subjects who are easily suggestible, such as small children, the validity of their answers may be jeopardized.

Although the wording of a question can inadvertently shape the content of an answer, it is often overlooked that deliberately leading questions are necessary parts of many questioning procedures, as exemplified by Hamlet's interview. The validity of leading questions depends on the topic and purpose of the investigation. Legal interrogators may on purpose pose leading questions in order to obtain information they suspect is being withheld. The burden of denial is then put on the subject, as with the question, 'When did you stop beating your wife?' Police officers and lawyers intentionally apply leading questions to test the consistency and reliability of a person's statements. Piaget used questions leading in wrong directions in order to test the strength of the child's concept of, for example, weight. We may also recall Bourdieu's use of leading questions in his active confrontational interview with the two young men, such as 'What were you doing, bugging him?' (Box 1.3). In Socrates' dialogue on love, he repeatedly employed leading questions with the intention of exposing the contradictions of Agathon's understanding of love and beauty and of leading Agathon to true insight.

In contrast to common opinion, the qualitative research interview is particularly well suited for employing leading questions to repeatedly check the reliability of the interviewees' answers, as well as to verify the interviewer's interpretations. Thus leading questions need not reduce the reliability of interviews, but may enhance it; rather than being used too much, deliberately leading questions are today probably applied too little in qualitative research interviews.

It should be noted that not only may the questions preceding an answer be leading, but the interviewer's own bodily and verbal responses, such as second questions following an answer, can act as positive or negative reinforcers for the answer given and thereby influence the subject's answers to further questions. We may also note that in questionnaires, the response alternatives lead the subjects' answers in specific directions when closing off the responses to answer either 'yes' or 'no' to a question, without a possibility of arguing that a question may be based upon a false dichotomy. Such leading questions close off the range of potential answers, exemplified by the question 'Which hand do you choose?' excluding answers where the subject does not want to choose either hand. An advantage of the qualitative research interview is that the interviewee has an open range of response possibilities, including a rejection of the premises of the interviewer's questions, such as the vocational pupil crossing discourses with the interviewer.

While the technical issue of using leading questions in an interview has been rather overemphasized, the leading effects of project-based research questions have received less attention. Recall the different kinds of answers obtained by a Rogerian, a Freudian and a Skinnerian approach in the imaginary interview on teasing and in the interview about grades (Chapters 4 and 5). A project's orienting of research questions determines what kind of answers may be obtained. The task is, again, not to avoid leading research questions, but to recognize the primacy of the question and attempt to make the orienting questions explicit, thereby providing the reader with the possibility of evaluating their influence on the research findings and of assessing the validity of the findings.

The fact that the issue of leading questions has received so much attention in interview research may be due to prevailing empiricist and positivist conceptions of knowledge. There may be a belief in a neutral observational access to an objective social reality independent of the investigator, implying that an interviewer collects verbal responses as a miner finds buried metals or a botanist collects plants in nature. In an alternative traveller view, which follows from a postmodern perspective on knowledge construction, the interview is a conversation in which the knowledge is constructed in and through an interpersonal relationship, co-authored and co-produced by interviewer and interviewee. The decisive issue is not whether to lead or not to lead, but where the interview questions lead, whether they lead to new, trustworthy and worthwhile knowledge.

Tensions of scientific and ethical responsibility

The search for interview knowledge of high scientific quality, with the interviewees' answers critically probed and alternative interpretations checked out, may in some cases conflict with ethical concerns of not harming the interviewee (Brinkmann and Kvale, 2005; Flick, 2007b, chap. 9). The dilemma of wanting as much knowledge as possible, while at the same time respecting the integrity of the interview subjects, is not easily solved.

Jette Fog (2004) has formulated the interviewer's ethical dilemma as follows: the researcher wants the interview to be as deep and probing as possible, with the risk of intruding upon the person, and on the other hand to be as respectful to the interview person as possible, with the risk of getting empirical material that only scratches the surface. In a study of living with cancer, a woman is interviewed and denies that she fears a return of the disease. She says that she is not afraid, and she appears happy and reasonable. However, as a skilled interviewer and therapist, Fog senses small signals to the contrary: The woman speaks very fast, her smile and the way she moves her hands is independent of her words. Her body is rigid and she does not listen to her own words. If the interviewer decides to respect the interviewee's words, and refrains from anything resembling therapeutic intervention, then the written interview will subsequently tell the story of a woman living peacefully with cancer. In this way valuable knowledge might be lost, which could only have been obtained by trying to get behind the apparent denial and defences of the interviewee. If society has an interest in finding out what it means to live with a deadly disease, then should the researcher perhaps try to go behind the face value of the woman's words? But what is in the interest of the woman? Perhaps it is best for her not to have her defences broken down, or maybe she will live a better life if she faces up to the reality of her disease?

Such dilemmas of conflicting scientific and ethical concerns cannot be solved by ethical rules, but will depend on the ethical experience and judgement of the researcher. In some cases, research options may exist where the described dilemma does not arise. If the research interview above had been a therapeutic interview, it would be part of the therapeutic process to go beyond the subject's apparent denials, and possibly open to hurtful self-confrontations, and as a side-effect obtain more thoroughly checked and penetrating knowledge than is ethically defensible in a research interview.

We shall conclude that there are no unequivocal quality criteria for research interviews. A good interview rests upon the craftsmanship of the researcher, which goes beyond a mastery of questioning techniques to encompass knowledge of the research topic, sensitivity to the social relation of interviewer and subject, and an awareness of epistemological and ethical aspects of research interviewing.

Key points

- The quality of the original interview is decisive for the quality of the analysis, verification and reporting of the interview.
- There are no fixed criteria for what constitutes a good interview, either when it comes to the scientific or the ethical quality: the evaluation of interview quality depends on the specific form, topic and purpose of the interview.
- Three general quality criteria for a good interview concern the richness of the interviewee's answers, the length of relevant answers and the clarification of the interviewee's statements.

- Three further, and more debatable, quality criteria for an ideal interview concern how well interpreted, verified and reported the interview-produced knowledge is in the interview situation itself.
- Qualification criteria for an interviewer include that he or she be knowledgeable, structuring, clear, gentle, sensitive, open, steering, critical, remembering and interpreting.
- Interview reports may be met with a series of external objections. An acquaintance with some of the common criticisms of interview research may assist the interviewer in taking such likely objections into account when conducting and reporting an interview investigation.
- The answer to the frequent question of leading questions is twofold: first, that deliberate leading questions are probably used too little in current interview research; and second, the decisive issue is not whether to lead or not to lead, but whether the questions lead to important knowledge.
- In some cases, criteria for the scientific quality of a research interview may be in conflict with ethical criteria of respect for the person of the interviewee.

Further reading

Issues of quality in qualitative research are addressed in these two works in more detail:

Flick, U. (2007b) *Managing Quality in Qualitative Research* (Book 8 of *The SAGE Qualitative Research Kit*). London: Sage.
Seale, C. (2004) 'Quality in qualitative research', in C. Seale, G. Gobo, J.F. Gubrium and D. Silverman (eds), *Qualitative Research Practice*. London: Sage, pp. 407–19.

8
Transcribing interviews

Oral and written language   92
Recording interviews   93
Transcribing interviews   94
Transcription reliability and validity   97
Computer tools for interview analysis   98

Chapter objectives
After reading this chapter, you should know more about

- the post-interview stages of working with the outcome of the interview: transcribing, analyzing, verifying and reporting the knowledge produced in the interview conversations;
- the transformation of the oral interview conversation to a written text as transcripts amenable to analysis;
- some principal differences between oral and written language;
- practical issues of recording and transcribing;
- reliability and validity of transcriptions; and
- computer programs facilitating interview analysis.

Oral and written language

The quality of interviewing is often discussed, whereas the quality of transcription is seldom addressed in qualitative research literature. This may be related to a traditional lack of attention among social scientists to the linguistic medium they work with. Rather than being a simple clerical task, transcription is an interpretative process, where the differences between oral speech and written texts give rise to a series of practical and principal issues.

By neglecting issues of transcription, the interview researcher's road to hell becomes paved with transcripts. The interview is an evolving face-to-face conversation between two persons; by transcription the direct face-to-face conversation becomes abstracted and fixated into a written form. Once the interview transcriptions have been made, they tend to be regarded as *the* solid rock-bottom empirical data of an interview project. In contrast, from a linguistic perspective the transcriptions are translations from an oral language to a written language, where the constructions on the way involve a series of judgements and decisions. A transcript is a translation from one narrative mode – oral discourse – into another narrative mode – written discourse. Oral speech and written texts entail different language games, and according to Ong (1982) also different cultures. The rules of the game differ; an eloquent speech may appear incoherent and repetitive in direct transcription, and an articulately argued article may sound boring when read aloud.

To transcribe means to transform, to change from one form to another. Attempts at verbatim interview transcriptions produce hybrids, artificial constructs that may be adequate for neither the lived oral conversation nor the formal style of written texts. Transcriptions are translations from an oral language to a written language; what is said in the hermeneutical tradition of translators also pertains to transcribers: *traduire traittori* – translators are traitors.

An interview is a live social interaction where the pace of the temporal unfolding, the tone of the voice and the bodily expressions are immediately available to the participants in the face-to-face conversation, but they are not accessible to the out-of-context reader of the transcript. The tape recording of the interview involves a first abstraction from the lived bodily presence of the conversing persons, with a loss of body language as posture and gestures. The transcription of the interview conversation to a written form involves a second abstraction, where the tone of the voice, the intonations and the breathing are lost. In short, transcripts are impoverished decontextualized renderings of interview conversations.

Recording interviews

Methods of recording interviews for documentation and later analysis include audiotape recording, videotape recording, note-taking and remembering. The common way of recording interviews has been with the use of a tape recorder. The interviewer can then concentrate on the topic and the dynamics of the interview. The words and their tone, pauses and the like are recorded in a permanent form that it is possible to return to again and again for re-listening. Today digital voice recorders are available; they provide a high acoustic quality and can record for many hours without interruption. The recordings can be transferred directly to a computer where they can be stored and played for analysis.

The first requirement for transcribing an interview is that it was in fact recorded. Some interviewers have painful memories of an exceptional interview where nothing got on the tape due to technical defects or, most often, human error. A second requirement for transcription is that the recorded conversation is audible to the transcriber. This may require that the interviewer takes measures to avoid background noise and is not afraid to ask a mumbling interviewee to speak up.

Video recordings offer a unique opportunity for analyzing the interpersonal interaction in an interview; the wealth of information, however, makes videotape analysis a time-consuming process. For ordinary interview projects, particularly those with many interviews and where the main interest is the content of what is said, video recordings may be too cumbersome for the analysis of the interview content. This said, video recordings of pilot interviews might be useful to sensitize interviewers to the importance of body language (see also Rapley, 2007, for more details).

An interview may also be recorded by a reflected use of the interviewer's remembrance, relying on his or her empathy and memory, and then writing down the main aspects of the interview after the session, sometimes assisted by notes taken during the interview. Taking extensive notes during an interview may, however, be distracting, interrupting the free flow of conversation. There are obvious limitations of the interviewer's remembrance, such as a rapid forgetting of exact linguistic formulations, whereas the bodily presence and the social atmosphere of the interview situation, lost on the tape, may remain in the background of memory. The interviewer's active listening and remembering may work as a selective filter, not only as a bias, but potentially also to retain those very meanings that are essential for the topic and the purpose of the interview. One might speculate that if tape recorders had been available in Freud's time, psychoanalytic theory might not have developed beyond infinite series of verbatim quotes from the patients, and psychoanalysis might today have remained confined to a small Viennese sect of psychoanalysts lost in a chaos of therapy tapes and disputes over their correct transcriptions.

Transcribing interviews

Transcribing the interviews from an oral to a written mode structures the interview conversations in a form amenable to closer analysis, and is in itself an initial analysis (see Rapley, 2007, for more details). The amount and form of transcribing depends on such factors as the nature of the material and the purpose of the investigation, the time and money available, and – not to be forgotten – the availability of a reliable and patient typist.

Time and resources for transcription

The time needed to transcribe an interview will depend on the quality of the recording, the typing experience of the transcriber and the demands for detail and exactitude. Transcribing large amounts of interview material is often a tiresome and stressing job, the stress being reduced by securing recordings of high acoustic quality. For the interviews in the grading study, an experienced secretary took about 5 hours to type verbatim a 1-hour interview. An interview of 1 hour results in 20 to 25 single-spaced pages, depending on the amount of speech and how it is set up in typing.

- *Who should transcribe?* The tapes are transcribed by a secretary in most inter-view studies. Investigators who emphasize the modes of communication and linguistic style may choose to do their own transcribing in order to secure the many details relevant to their specific analysis. Mishler (1986, cf. also 1991) describes how he would let a secretary do a rough transcription of his inter-views and then select a few interviews for extensive narrative analysis. He would transcribe these interviews himself, with linguistic annotations such as in the craftsman narrative (Box 6.2). Researchers who transcribe their own interviews will learn much about their own interviewing style; to some extent they will have the social and emotional aspects of the interview situation pres-ent or reawakened during transcription, and will already have started the analysis of the meaning of what was said.
- *Transcription procedure.* Transcribing from tape to text involves a series of technical and interpretational issues – in particular, verbatim oral versus written style – for which there are few standard rules, but rather a series of choices to be made. There is one basic rule in transcription: state explicitly in the report how the transcriptions were made. This should preferably be based on written instructions to the transcribers. If there are several transcribers for the interviews of a single study, care should be taken that they use the same procedures for typing. If this is not done, it will be difficult to make linguistic cross-comparisons among the interviews.
- *Use of transcriptions.* Although there is no standard form or code for tran-scription of research interviews, there are some standard choices to be made. Should the statements be transcribed verbatim and word by word, retaining frequent repetitions, noting 'mh'-s and the like, or should the interview be transformed into a more formal, written style? Sampling in interview studies does not only concern selection of subjects, transcription involves the sam-pling of which of the multiple dimensions of oral interview conversations are to be selected for written transcription; for example, should pauses, emphases in intonation, and emotional expressions like laughter and sighing be includ-ed? And if pauses are to be included, how much detail should be indicated? There are no correct, standard answers to such questions; the answers will depend on the intended use of the transcript, for example, whether for a detailed linguistic conversational analysis or for reporting the subject's accounts in a readable public story.

Box 8.1   Transcription for conversation analysis

E: Oh honey that was a lovely luncheon I shoulda ca:lled you s:soo(:ner but

     I:)I:(lo:ved it.

M: (((f)) Oh:::) ((   )

E: It w's just deli:ghtfu(:l.)

M: (Well)=

M: I w's gla(d   you) (came).)

E: ('nd yer f:) friends) 're so da:rli:ng,=

M: =Oh:::(:it w'z)

E: (e-that P)a:t isn't she a do:(:ll?)

M: (iYe)h isn't she pretty.

        (.)

E: *Oh*: she's a beautiful girl.=

M: =Yeh I think she's a pretty gir(l.=

E: (En' that Reinam'n::

        (.)

E: *She* SCA:RES me.

Source: Heritage (1984), cited from Have (1999, p. 4).

Transcription Conventions:

(A *single left bracket* indicates the point of overlap onset.

) A *single right bracket* indicates the point at which an utterance-part terminates vis-à-vis another.

= *Equal signs*, one at the end of one line and one at the beginning of a next, indicate no 'gap' between the two lines.

(.) A dot in parentheses indicates a tiny 'gap' within or between utterances.

:: Colons indicate prolongation of the immediately prior sound. Multiple colons indicate a more prolonged sound.

word *underscoring* indicates some form of stress, via pitch and/or amplitude; an alternative method is to print the stressed part in *italics*.

WORD *Upper case* indicates especially loud sounds relative to the surrounding talk.

( ) *Empty parentheses* indicate the transcriber's inability to hear what was said.

(( )) *Double parentheses* indicate the transcriber's descriptions rather than transcriptions.

Source: adapted from Have (1999, Appendix).

The text in Box 8.1 may at first sight appear rather incomprehensible. It is a transcription of a sequence of telephone conversation, presented here to demonstrate the complexities of transcription for special purposes, in this case for a conversation analysis, to be depicted in Chapter 9. We may also note that Mishler used some of the annotations in his rendering of a narrative interview with a craftsman (Box 6.2). Such specialized forms of transcriptions are neither feasible, nor necessary, for the meaning analysis of large interview texts in common interview projects. Whereas if the focus is on the linguistic style and the social interaction in a research interview, or in a doctor–patient interview, the pauses, overlaps and intonations of the speech interaction may be of key importance. Transcriptions in detail, such as in Box 8.1, may also sensitize interviewers to the finer points of interview interaction.

The issue of how detailed a transcription should be is illustrated by an interview sequence on competition for grades, which in Denmark is a negative behaviour that many pupils hesitate to admit to:

Interviewer: Does it influence the relationship between the pupils that the grades are there?
Pupil: No, no – no, one does not look down on anyone who gets bad grades that is not done. I do not believe that: well, it may be that there are some who do it, but I don't.
Interviewer: Does that mean there is no competition in the class?
Pupil: That's right. There is none.

At face value, this boy says that one does not look down on pupils with low grades and confirms the interviewer's interpretation that there is no competition for grades in the class. A critical reading of the passage may, however, lead to the opposite conclusion – the repeated denials of looking down on other pupils may be interpreted as perhaps meaning the opposite of what was manifestly said. If the above interview sequence had not been transcribed verbatim, but rephrased into a briefer form such as 'One does not look down on others with low grades nor compete for grades', the potential reinterpretation of the manifest meaning of the statement into its opposite could not have taken place.

Transcription reliability and validity

The constructive nature of transcripts is apparent when taking a closer look at their reliability and validity.

Reliability
Technically regarded, it is an easy check to have two persons independently transcribe the same passage from a taped interview, and then have a computer program list and count the number of words that differ between the two transcriptions. Such a simple quantitative reliability check of the correspondence between the two transcriptions may be shocking to the interview researcher and hurt the professional honour of experienced typists.

Listening again to the tape might show that some discrepancies are due to poor recording quality, with mishearing and misinterpretations of hardly audible passages. Other divergences may not be unequivocally solved, as for example: Where does a sentence end? Where is there a pause? How long is a silence before it becomes a pause in a conversation? Does a specific pause belong to the subject or to the interviewer? And if the emotional aspects of the conversation are included, for instance 'tense voice', 'giggling', 'nervous laughter', and so on, the intersubjective reliability of the transcription could develop into a research project of its own. The transcription of the telephone conversation for a conversational analysis in Box 8.1 indicates the complexities of a precise translation from oral speech to written text.

Validity

Ascertaining the validity of the interview transcripts is more intricate than assuring their reliability. Transcribing involves translating from an oral language, with its own set of rules, to a written language with another set of rules. Transcripts are not copies or representations of some original reality, they are interpretative constructions that are useful tools for given purposes. Transcripts are decontextualized conversations; they are abstractions, as topographical maps are abstractions from the original landscape from which they are derived. Maps emphasize some aspects of the countryside and omit others, the selection of features depending on the intended use.

Correspondingly, the question 'What is the correct valid transcription?' cannot be answered – there is no true, objective transformation from the oral to the written mode. A more constructive question is 'What is a useful transcription for my research purposes?' Thus verbatim descriptions are necessary for linguistic analyses; the inclusion of pauses, repetitions and tone of voice may also be relevant for psychological interpretations of, for example, level of anxiety or the meaning of denials. On the other hand, transforming the conversation into a literary style may highlight nuances of a statement and facilitate communication of the meaning of the subject's stories to readers (see also Flick, 2007b, for reliability and validity).

Computer tools for interview analysis

Once the interviews have been transcribed, they become available for structuring and analysis by a variety of computer programs. Among novices to the trade there may be a belief that the intricate analysis of their interviews will be taken care of by a computer program. The marketing of computer programs for textual analysis may feed well into such high expectations, for example:

Qualitative research is a challenge! You are faced with rich data from interviews, focus groups, observations, surveys, profiles or web searches. How do you make sense of it and do justice to it? How do you find and explain patterns, identify themes and powerfully deliver your results? Meet the challenge! XXX offers the world's leading qualitative solutions for researchers.

Program developers themselves and textbook authors may promise less about computer programs for textual analysis: 'They are not a substitute for thought, but they are a strong aid for thought. … Computers don't analyze data; people do' (Weitzman and Miles, 1995, p. 3).

Computer programs facilitate the analysis of interview transcripts. They replace the time-demanding 'cut-and-paste' approach to hundreds of pages of transcripts with 'electronic scissors'. The programs are aids for structuring the interview material for further analysis; the task and the responsibility of interpretation remain with the researcher. The computer programs allow for such operations as writing memos, writing reflections on the interviews for later analyses, coding, searching for key words, doing word counts, and making graphic displays. Some of the programs allow for on-screen coding and taking notes while reading the transcripts. It should be noted that several of these tasks may also be taken care of by the common word-processing programs.

The most common form of computer analysis today is coding, or categorization, of the interview statements, to be discussed in the following chapter. By coding, the researcher first reads through the transcripts and codes the relevant passages; then with the aid of code-and-retrieve programs the coded passages can be retrieved and inspected over again, with options of recoding and of combining codes. Existing computer programs are well adapted for coding strategies, whereas the many other forms of interview analysis, such as narrative and discursive analysis, figure less in the computer-assisted programs for textual analysis. There is thus a danger that the ready availability of computer programs for coding can have the effect that coding becomes a preferred shortcut to analysis, at the expense of a rich variety of modes of interview analyses, to be presented in the following chapter.

While most computer programs today work with written texts, newer forms exist that deal directly with the sound recording. The investigator can listen directly to the interview interaction, code it, and write associations or interpretations on the text screen and later immediately get back to the coded sound sequence. Working directly with the sound will save the time and money for transcribing entire interviews, as well as overstep many of the problems of transcription discussed above and secure the researcher a close contact with the original oral discourse. Smaller passages to be reported or analyzed more intensively may then be selected for transcription (see Gibbs, 2007, for more details).

▤ Key points

- While the quality of interviewing has been discussed intensively, the quality of interview transcriptions has been a neglected issue.
- Oral conversations and written texts are linguistically quite different discourses, and their divergences should be kept in mind when transcribing.
- The reliability and validity of transcriptions are generally neglected. If these issues are addressed, the interpretative and constructive nature of transcription will appear.
- The reliability of transcription may be improved by securing the quality of the sound recording and by providing clear instructions for the mode of transcription.
- No valid transcription of an oral account exists, but a variety of forms of transcribing, which will be valid for different uses of the transcripts.
- Computer programs are available that may facilitate the analysis of the interviews. While most programs work with transcribed texts, there are also programs where the computer analysis may be conducted directly with the sound recording.
- Computer programs are tools for analysis; the challenges and the responsibility of the analysis remains with the researcher.

Further reading

Transcription in general and its quality in particular are issues of the following sources:

Flick, U. (2007b) *Managing Quality in Qualitative Research* (Book 8 of *The SAGE Qualitative Research Kit*). London: Sage.

Gibbs, G. (2007) *Analyzing Qualitative Data.* (Book 6 of *The SAGE Qualitative Research Kit*). London: Sage.

Mishler, E.G. (1991) 'Representing discourse: the rhetoric of transcription', *Journal of Narrative and Life History*, 1: 255–80.

Poland, B.D. (2002) 'Transcription quality', in J.F. Gubrium and J.A. Holstein (eds) (2002) *Handbook of Interview Research*. Thousand Oaks, CA: Sage, pp. 629–49.

Rapley, T. (2007) *Doing Conversation, Discourse and Document Analysis* (Book 7 of *The SAGE Qualitative Research Kit*). London: Sage.

Weitzman, E.A. and Miles, M.B. (1995) *Computer Programs for Qualitative Data Analysis*. Thousand Oaks, CA: Sage.

9
Analyzing interviews

Integrating interview analysis in an interview inquiry   101
Modes of analysis   103
Interview analyses focusing on meaning   104
Interview analyses focusing on language   109
Interview analysis as bricolage   115
Interview analysis as theoretical reading   117

Chapter objectives
After reading this chapter you should

- have an overview of analytic tools for analyzing interview texts;
- as interviewer be already sensitized, when conducting and transcribing your interviews, to be aware of the specific demands that different modes of analysis pose on your interviews and transcriptions;
- see the need for integrating the analysis throughout the entire interview project;
- know modes of analysis that primarily focus on the meanings expressed by the subjects;
- know modes of analysis that mainly focus on the linguistic form of the subjects' accounts; and
- be familiar with a common bricolage, where the researcher mixes different types of analysis, as well as a theoretical reading of the interviews.

Integrating interview analysis in an interview inquiry

When teaching at workshops on qualitative research, one may sometimes receive a question like this: *'How shall I find a method to analyze the 1,000 pages of interview transcripts I have collected?'*

The answer is simple: 'Too much and too late!' First, 1,000 pages of transcripts are generally too much to handle in a meaningful way for a single researcher. Second, it is too late to start thinking of analysis after the interviews have been conducted and transcribed. The method of analysis should not only be given thought in advance of the interviewing, but may also, to varying degrees, be built into the interview situation itself. A clarification of the meaning of what is said may there take the simple form of 'I understand that the meaning of what you just said is....' The researcher may further attempt to confirm or reject his or her interpretations during the interview. With such interpreting 'as you go', considerable parts of the analysis are 'pushed forward' into the interview situation itself. The later analysis then becomes not only easier and more amenable, but will also rest on more secure ground.

Box 9.1   Six steps of analysis

A first step is when *subjects describe* their life world during the interview. They spontaneously tell what they experience, feel and do in relation to a topic. There is little interpretation or explanation from either the interviewees or the interviewer.

A second step would be that the *subjects themselves discover* new relationships during the interview, see new meanings in what they experience and do so on the basis of their spontaneous descriptions, free of interpretation by the interviewer. For example, a pupil, describing the effects of grading, comes to think of how the grades further a destructive competition among pupils.

In a third step, the *interviewer, during the interview, condenses and interprets* the meaning of what the interviewee describes, and 'sends' the meaning back. The interviewee then has the opportunity to reply, for example, 'I did not mean that' or 'That was precisely what I was trying to say' or 'No, that was not quite what I felt. It was more like ... ' This process ideally continues until there is only one possible interpretation left, or it is established that the subject has multiple, and possibly contradictory, understandings of a theme. This form of interviewing implies an ongoing 'on-the-line interpretation' with the possibility of an 'on-the-spot' confirmation or disconfirmation of the interviewer's interpretations. The result can then be a 'self-correcting' interview.

In a fourth step, the *recorded interview is analyzed by the interviewer* alone, or with co-researchers. The interview is usually structured for analysis by transcription and with computer programs for textual analysis. The analysis proper involves developing the meanings of the interviews, bringing the subjects' own understanding into the light as well as providing new perspectives from the researcher. A variety of analytical tools focusing on the meaning and the linguistic form of the texts are available.

(Continued)

(Continued)

A fifth step would be a *re-interview*. When the researcher has analyzed the interview texts, he or she may give the interpretations back to the subjects. In a continuation of a 'self-correcting' interview, the subjects then get an opportunity to comment on the interviewer's interpretations as well as to elaborate on their own original statements, as a form of 'membership validation'.

A possible sixth step would be to extend the continuum of description and interpretation to include *action*, by subjects beginning to act on new insights they have gained during their interview. In such cases, the research interview may approximate a therapeutic interview. The changes can also be brought about by collective actions in a larger social setting such as action research, where researcher and subjects together act on the basis of the knowledge produced in the interviews.

Box 9.1 presents six steps of a continuum from description to interpretation and action, which do not necessarily presuppose each other. The first three steps of description, discovery and interpretation throughout the interview process were outlined in Chapter 5. I shall now turn to analytic tools available at the fourth step of analyzing the transcribed interview.

Modes of analysis

The following presentation will disappoint those who expect magical tools that finally uncover the treasures of meaning hidden in their many pages of transcripts. No standard method exists, no *via regia*, to arrive at essential meanings and deeper implications of what is said in an interview. Such a search for techniques of analysis may be a quest for a shortcut in the form of a 'technological fix' of the researcher's task of analyzing and constructing meaning. Some common approaches to the analysis of the meaning of interview texts – involving different technical procedures – do exist, however. The techniques of analysis are tools, useful for some purposes, relevant for some types of interviews, and suited for some researchers.

The present chapter describes a toolbox available to the interview craftsman for the analysis of interviews. These tools do not by themselves find the meaning of hundreds of pages of interview transcripts the researcher who applies the tools does. The quality of the analysis rests upon his or her craftsmanship, knowledge of the research topic, sensitivity for the medium he or she is working with – language – and mastery of analytic tools available for analyzing the meanings expressed in language. The following overview of the toolbox and descriptions of

TABLE 9.1 Modes of interview analysis

Analyses focusing on meaning:

> Meaning coding
> Meaning condensation
> Meaning interpretation

Analyses focusing on language:

> Linguistic analysis
> Conversation analysis
> Narrative analysis
> Discursive analysis
> Deconstruction

Bricolage
Theoretical reading

main tools can assist interviewers in choosing modes of analysis adequate for their project. Some of the analytic tools, such as coding, have been developed through practice without a theoretical basis; some have been inspired by philosophical traditions, such as phenomenology and hermeneutics; whereas some such as discursive and deconstructive analysis, have been built directly upon specific epistemological positions.

Some key approaches to the analysis of interview texts are presented in Table 9.1. They are grouped into analyses that mainly focus on the meaning of what is said, and analyses that mainly focus on the linguistic forms whereby meanings are expressed. In addition, there is analysis as bricolage, an eclectic combination of multiple forms of analysis, and a theoretically informed reading of the interviews as a significant mode of analysis. Some of the analyses come close to a miner metaphor of interviewing, such as meaning coding and condensation, which attempt to bring out what is already there in the texts. Other analyses are more in line with a traveller metaphor, such as linguistic, conversation and discursive analysis, which focus on the language medium of the stories told, generally without taking a position on whether the conversations refer to any objective data or essential meanings. For the varieties of meaning interpretation and narrative analysis, both metaphors may apply.

Interview analyses focusing on meaning

Meaning and language are interwoven; in the practice of interview analysis the focus on meaning versus linguistic form does imply rather different techniques, however. First some modes of analysis focusing on meaning of texts will be outlined; they involve coding, condensation and interpretation of meaning.

Meaning coding

Coding and categorizing were early approaches to the analysis of texts in the social sciences. Coding involves attaching one or more keywords to a text segment in order to permit later identification of a statement, whereas categorization entails a more systematic conceptualization of a statement, opening for quantification; the two terms are, however, often used interchangeably. In various forms, coding is a key aspect of content analysis, grounded theory and computer-assisted analysis of interview texts.

Content analysis

This is a technique for a systematic quantitative description of the manifest content of communication. It was developed for the study of enemy propaganda during the second World War and has since been used extensively for media analysis. The coding of a text's meaning into categories made it possible to quantify how often specific themes were addressed in a text, and the frequency of themes could then be compared and correlated with other measures. Coding is also a key feature of the *grounded theory* approach to qualitative research introduced by Glaser and Strauss in 1967. Here open coding refers to 'The process of breaking down, examining, comparing, conceptualizing and categorizing data' (Strauss and Corbin, 1990, p. 61). In contrast to content analysis, the codes in a grounded theory approach do not need to be quantified, but enter into a qualitative analysis of the relations to other codes and to context and action consequences. Coding has also become a key feature of the new programs for computer-assisted analysis of interviews (Weitzman and Miles, 1995).

By categorization, the meaning of long interview statements is reduced to a few simple categories. When coding into fixed categories, the occurrence and non-occurrence of a phenomenon can be expressed by a simple '+' or '−'. The strength of an opinion can also be indicated with a single number on a scale of, for example, 1 to 7. Categorization thus reduces and structures large interview texts into a few tables and figures. The categories can be developed in advance or they can arise ad hoc during the analysis; they may be taken from theory or from the vernacular, as well as from the interviewees' own idioms. Categorizing the interviews of an investigation can provide an overview of large amounts of transcripts, and facilitate comparisons and hypothesis testing.

The analysis of the interviews on grades illustrates one form of categorization. The 30 pupil interviews, transcribed into 762 pages, were categorized in order to test the hypothesis that using grades to measure learning affects learning and social relations in school. Figure 9.1 depicts eight subcategories of one main dimension of a grade perspective, 'Relationshipship with the teacher'. The categories were taken from educational literature and pilot interviews, and defined (for example: 'Bluffing – the pupil attempts to give the impression that he knows more than he knows, with the purpose of obtaining better grades' and 'Wheedling – the pupil

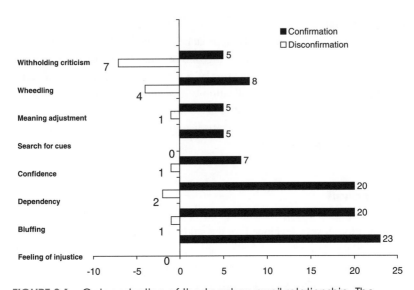

FIGURE 9.1 Categorization of the teacher–pupil relationship. The number of the 30 pupils interviewed who confirmed occurrence of a grading behaviour and attitude is shown on the right, and the number who disconfirmed a grading behaviour and attitude is on the left. As several pupils had no statements, or vague statements, regarding a category, the sum of direct confirmations and disconfirmations is less than 30.

attempts to win the sympathy of the teacher with the purpose of obtaining better grades'). Two coders independently categorized the 30 interviews, and their coding was combined. Figure 9.1 depicts how many of the 30 pupils confirmed or disconfirmed each of the eight subcategories of the dimension 'Relationship with the teacher', generally supporting the hypothesis that grades influences social relations in school (Kvale, 1980, 1996b).

Implications for interviewing   With categorization involving either/or decisions, it is preferable with precise pre-interview definitions of the categories and careful probing during the interview to ascertain how the statements may be categorized. When the codes or categories are not to be developed until interviewing and analysis, it is important during the interviews to obtain rich descriptions of the specific phenomena to be coded or categorized.

Meaning condensation

Meaning condensation entails an abridgement of the meanings expressed by the interviewees into shorter formulations. Long statements are compressed into briefer statements in which the main sense of what is said is rephrased in a few words. I shall here exemplify one form of meaning condensation developed by Giorgi (1975) on the basis of phenomenological philosophy. The thematic purpose of his study was to investigate what constitutes learning for ordinary people in their everyday activities. The methodological purpose was to demonstrate how one deals systematically with data that remain expressed in terms of ordinary language and how rigour and discipline can be applied in data analysis without necessarily transforming the data into quantitative expressions.

Table 9.2 demonstrates how an interview about learning was subjected to meaning condensation. The analysis involves five steps. First, the complete interview is read through to get a sense of the whole. Then, the natural 'meaning units' of the text, such as they are expressed by the subjects, are determined by the researcher. Third, the theme that dominates a natural meaning unit is restated by the researcher as simply as possible, thematizing the statements from the subject's viewpoint as understood by the researcher. Table 9.2 depicts this third step of analysis. The fourth step consists of interrogating the meaning units in terms of the specific purpose of the study. In the fifth step, the essential, non-redundant themes of the entire interview are tied together into a descriptive statement.

This form of meaning condensation can serve to analyze extensive and often complex interview texts by looking for natural meaning units and explicating their main themes. These themes may thereafter be subject to more extensive interpretations and theoretical analyses. Giorgi thus points out the importance of interpersonal relations by learning, which emerged in this study – a phenomenon that was rather neglected in the theories of learning at the time. (For further developments of the method, see Fischer and Wertz, 1979, and Giorgi and Giorgi, 2003.) It should also be noted that meaning condensation is not confined to a phenomenological approach and is also applied in other qualitative studies (Tesch, 1990).

Implications for interviewing   For a phenomenologically based meaning condensation it becomes paramount to obtain rich and nuanced descriptions of the phenomena investigated in the subjects' everyday language. The interviewer's theories of the subject matter should be 'put into brackets' during the interviewing.

Meaning interpretation

The interpretation of the meaning of interview texts goes beyond a structuring of the manifest meanings of what is said to deeper and more critical interpretations of the text. Meaning interpretation is prevalent in the humanities, such as in a   **107**

TABLE 9.2   Meaning condensation

Natural unit	Central theme
The first thing that comes to mind is what I learned about interior decorating from Myrtis. She was telling me about the way you see things. Her view of looking at different rooms has been altered. She told me that when you come into a room you don't usually notice how many vertical and horizontal lines there are, at least consciously, you don't notice. And yet, if you were to take someone who knows what's going on in the field of interior decoration, they would intuitively feel there was the right number of vertical and horizontal lines.	Role of vertical and horizontal lines in interior decorating
So, I went home, and I started looking at the lines in our living room, and I counted the number of horizontal and vertical lines, many of which I had never realized were lines before. A beam ... I had never really thought of that as vertical before, just as a protrusion from the wall. (Laughs) design: I found out what was wrong with our living room many, too many, horizontal lines and not enough vertical. So I started trying to move things around and change the way it looked. I did this by moving several pieces of furniture and taking out several knick-knacks, de-emphasizing certain lines, and ... it really looked differently to me.	S looks for vertical and horizontal lines in her home. S found too many horizontal lines in living room and succeeded in changing its appearance.
It's interesting because my husband came home several hours later and I said 'Look at the living room, it's all different'. Not knowing this, that I had picked up, he didn't look at it in the same way I did. He saw things were moved, but he wasn't able to verbalize that there was a de-emphasis on the horizontal lines and more of an emphasis on the vertical. So I felt I learned something.	Husband confirms difference not knowing why.

Source: Giorgi (1975).

critic's interpretations of a poem or a film, and in psychoanalytical interpretations of patients' dreams. The interpreter goes beyond what is directly said to work out structures and relations of meaning not immediately apparent in a text. In contrast to the de-contextualization of statements by categorization, interpretation re-contextualizes the statements within broader frames of reference. As compared to the text reduction techniques of categorization and condensation, interpretations often lead to a text expansion, with the outcome formulated in far more words than the original statements interpreted.

One example of meaning interpretation was given by the evaluation of Hamlet's interview in Chapter 7 (see Box 7.1). Different readings of the interview lead to rather different meanings, such as whether Hamlet's leading questions lead to unreliable or reliable knowledge, and whether it is Polonius or Hamlet who is fooled in the interview. No systematic method of meaning interpretation was in play here.

Within a hermeneutic tradition of text interpretation in the humanities, principles have been sought for arriving at valid interpretations of religious, legal and literary texts (see Palmer, 1969). Hermeneutics does not involve any step-by-step method, but is an explication of general principles found useful in a long tradition of interpreting texts. Thus interpretation of a text is characterized by a *hermeneutical circle,* where the meaning of a text is established through a process in which the meanings of the separate passages are determined by the global meaning of the text as it is anticipated. Re-reading of the single passages may again change the first anticipated global meaning of the text, which again alters the meaning of the single passages, and so on. In principle, such a hermeneutic text interpretation is an infinite process, whereas in practice it ends when a sensible coherent meaning has been arrived at.

Interpretations of meaning are sometimes steeped in mistrust of what is said. Hamlet's interview was thus read as expressing a pervasive distrust of the words and acts of the other players, leading to conversations of 'per indirections find directions out'. Within a 'hermeneutics of suspicion', statements are critically interpreted as meaning something else than what is manifestly said, such as when a psychoanalytic interpreter looks for unconscious forces beneath what is said, or Marxist interpreters look for ideological class interests behind political statements.

Implications for interviewing and transcription   For deep and critical interpretations of meaning, rich and nuanced descriptions in the interviews are advantageous, as well as critical interpretative questions during the interview. For some types of interpretation, detailed verbatim descriptions may be necessary, such as when critically reading of a pupil's many denials of competition in Chapter 8.

Interview analyses focusing on language

A good craftsman is familiar with the material he works with and the tools for working with it. The medium, or the material, with which interviewers work is language. The interview process occurs through speech, and the interview products are presented in words. During the last few decades, qualitative social science researchers have been influenced by the linguistic turn in philosophy, and they have started to use linguistic tools developed in the humanities to analyze their linguistic material. These include linguistic analysis, narrative analysis, conversation analysis, discourse analysis and deconstruction.

Linguistic analysis

Interviewing is linguistic interaction, and the product of the interview is a language text. A linguistic analysis addresses the characteristic uses of language in an interview, the use of grammar and linguistic forms. A linguistic analysis may thus study an interviewee's use of an active and a passive voice, of personal and impersonal pronouns, the temporal and spatial references, the implied speaker and listener positions and the use of metaphors.

An example from the grading study may indicate the importance of linguistic form. The analysis did not follow from any linguistic competence of the researcher, but arose as a practical problem by categorizing the pupils' statements. While most grading behaviours were commonly described in a first-person form, such as 'I find the grades unfair', 'I bluffed the teacher', a few activities, such as wheedling, were always described in a third-person form as 'They wheedled' or 'One wheedled'. If I had then been more sensitive to the differential use of personal pronouns, we might, in the interviews, have probed more into such vague expressions as 'one wheedles' and clarified whether it referred to the speaker or to other pupils. While a method problem when categorizing the statements as referring to the interviewee or to the other pupils, the diverging use of personal pronouns was of importance to the research topic as one of the many indications of the contrasting social acceptance of bluffing versus wheedling among the Danish high school pupils.

Attention to the linguistic features of an interview may contribute to both generating and verifying the meaning of statements. While the significance of the different use of grammatical forms such as the above example of personal pronouns may follow from common sense, a linguistically trained reader would immediately look for the linguistic expressions and be able to bring out nuances that may be important for interpreting the meaning of a statement. Arguments in favour of applying the techniques of linguistics as a 'statistics' of qualitative research have even been put forward (Jensen, 1989). With more attention to the linguistic medium of interview research, we may perhaps see social researchers use linguistics as consultants when faced with interview texts, corresponding to the commonplace use of statistical consultants when analyzing numbers.

Implications for interviewing and transcription Attention to linguistic form may improve the preciseness of interview questions, as suggested in Box 5.4, and further sensitivity in listening to the subjects' use of language. To carry out systematic linguistic analyses of the interview interaction, detailed verbatim transcription and also linguistic training is necessary.

Conversation analysis

Conversation analysis is a method for studying talk in interaction. It investigates the structure and the process of linguistic interaction whereby intersubjective understanding is created and maintained. Inspired by ethnomethodology, conversation analysis implies a pragmatic theory of language, it is about what words and sentences do; the meaning of a statement is the role it plays in a specific social practice. Conversation analysis started with studies of telephone conversations by Sacks and co-workers in the 1960s, and has since been used for a wide variety of talk in action, such as doctor–patient interactions, therapy sessions and news interviews.

Conversation analysis examines the minute details of talk-in-interaction, which has become widely accessible with the advent of tape recorders. It focuses on the sequencing of talk, in particular upon turn-taking sequences and repair of turn-taking errors. The centre of attention is not the speakers' intentions in a statement, but on what a specific speech segment accomplishes. Consequently, the outcome of the conversation analysis of the telephone conversation transcribed in Box 8-1 was:

> E apparently has called M after having visited her. She provides a series of
> 'assessments' of the occasion, and M's friends who were present. E's assess-
> ments are relatively intense and produced in a sort of staccato manner. The
> first two, on the occasion and the friends in general are accepted with Oh-
> prefaced short utterances, cut-off when E continues … The assessments of
> Pat are endorsed by M with 'yeh', followed by a somewhat lower level
> assessment. 'a do:ll?' with 'Yeh isn't she pretty' and 'Oh: she's a beautiful
> girl.', with 'Yeh I think she's a pretty girl.' …The 'work' that is done with these
> assessments and receipts can be glossed as 'showing and receiving grati-
> tude and appreciation, gracefully'. (ten Have, 1999, pp. 4–5)

Conversational analysis thus sticks rather close to the verbal interaction of the talkers, forgoing interpretations in depth. The labour-intensive transcription and the minute analyses of the speech sequences rules out conversation analysis as a general method for analysis of large amounts of interview material. Conversation analysis may, however, be relevant for selected significant parts of an interview, and it may also be useful in the training of interviewers, to make them aware of the subtleties of the interaction in the interviews.

Implications for transcription   Here there are no specific requirements to interviews since any verbal exchange can be made the subject of conversational analysis. As will have appeared from the transcription in Box 8.1, there are, nevertheless, very specific and elaborate requirements for how interviews are to be transcribed in order to be amenable to conversational analysis (see also Rapley, 2007).

Narrative analysis

A narrative is a story. Narrative analyses focus on the meaning and the linguistic form of texts, they address the temporal and social structures and the plots of interview stories. The narrative structures of stories people tell have been worked out in the humanities, starting with Propp's analysis of the structures of Russian fairy tales in the 1920s, and followed up decades later by Greimas and Labov. In the structure of a fairy tale, the main subject position may be taken by the prince as the actor, who seeks the object in the form of the princess. On his way, the prince encounters opponents as well as helpers, and after overcoming many obstacles, the prince receives from the king the princess and half his kingdom. Greimas used this structure to work out an actant model pertaining to narrative structures in a variety of genres (see also Gibbs, 2007).

The analysis of an interview can take the form of narration, as a continuation of the story told by the interviewee. Narrative analysis focuses on the stories told during an interview and works out their structures and their plots. If no stories are told spontaneously, a coherent narrative may be constructed from the many episodes spread throughout an interview. The analysis may also be a reconstruction of the many tales told by the different subjects into a 'typical' narrative as a richer, more condensed and coherent story than the scattered stories of single interviews. As with meaning condensation, narrative analysis will tend to stay within the vernacular.

A narrative sequence from Mishler's interview with a furniture craftsman-artist dropping out of the woodworking program at school was presented in Box 6.2. We may also note that the interview on learning interior decorating (Table 9.2) had the spontaneous form of a narrative, which Giorgi did not address by his meaning condensation of the interview. Chapter 4 on designing an interview study was introduced by a constructed narrative of successive emotional deterioration, followed by an idealized story of a linear progression through seven stages of an interview inquiry.

Implications for interviewing and transcription   Interviewing for narratives was described in Chapter 6, where questioning for concrete episodes and the following up of the subjects' spontaneous stories, elaborating their temporal and social structures and plots, were emphasized. In transcription one may experiment with the textual layout in ways to make the narrative form accessible, such as with the stanzas in Mishler's craftsman story (see Gibbs, 2007; Rapley, 2007, for more details).

Discourse analysis

Discourse analysis focuses on how truth effects are created within discourses, which are neither true nor false. Foucault's (1972) analysis of the power relations of discourses has inspired later forms of discourse analysis. Discourses are discontinuous practices, which cross each other and sometimes touch, while just as often ignoring or excluding each other. In Chapter 7, an interview sequence was presented, which, inspired by discourse analysis, was analyzed as a crossing of swords between the diverging discourses of learning by the interviewee and the electronics pupil.

In discourse analysis the talk itself has primacy, the focus is on how the talk is constructed and what the social consequences are of the different discursive presentations of a social situation:

> Participant's discourse or social texts are approached in *their own right* and not as a secondary route 'beyond' the text like attitudes, events or cognitive processes. Discourse is treated as a potent, action-oriented medium, not a transparent information channel. Crucial questions for traditional social psychological research thus cease to be relevant. For example, we are not asking whether a sample of people are revealing their 'genuine' attitudes to ethnic minorities, or whether fan's descriptions of what happens on the soccer terraces are 'accurate'. (Potter and Wetherell, 1987, p. 160)

From a discourse-analytic perspective, some common objections to the validity of research interviewing thus dissolve. This concerns the question of authentic personal meanings – 'How do you know you get to know what the interviewee really means?' – as well as the objective reality question – 'How do you know that your interviewee gives a true description of the objective situation?' A persistent objection concerning the reliability of interviewing has been that different interviewers get different results. If subjects present themselves differently to different interviewers, and also change their opinions during the interchange, then interviews do not produce reliable, objective, knowledge.

These objections may be based upon conceptions of the research topic, such as attitudes or presentation of the self, as expressions of an essential stable core person. In contrast, a discursive understanding treats attitudes and the self as interrelationally constituted. These phenomena may vary in different situations with different interviewers, and interviewing is a sensitive method to investigate the varying social presentations of the self. Thus, according to the differing epistemological conceptions of attitudes and the self – as stable authentic essences, or as socially constituted and more or less fluid ones – the interview appears either as a highly unreliable or as a finely tuned valid method.

Implications for interviewing   While discourse analysis may be applied to common interviews, such as the one described as discourses 'crossing swords', a specific discursive interviewing will focus on variation and diversity, and on the active participation of the interviewer in the discourse, as shown in Chapter 6. The search for real inner meanings and objective presentations of external reality dissolve in wild goose chases.

Deconstruction

The concept of 'deconstruction' was introduced by Derrida as a combination of 'destruction' and 'construction'. Deconstruction involves destructing one understanding of a text and opening it for construction of other understandings. The focus is not on what the person who uses a concept means, but on what the concept says and does not say. It is affiliated with a critical 'hermeneutics of suspicion', but in line with conversational and discursive analysis, it does not search for any underlying genuine or stable meaning hidden beneath a text. Meaning is understood in relation to an infinite network of other words in a language.

A deconstructive reading tears a text apart, unsettling the concepts it takes for granted; it concentrates on the tensions and breaks off a text, on what a text purports to say and what it comes to say, as well as what is not said in the text, on what is excluded by the use of the text's concepts. A deconstructive reading reveals the presuppositions and internal hierarchies of a text and lays open the binary oppositions built into modern thought and language, such as true/false, real/unreal, subjective/objective. Deconstruction does not only decompose a text, but also leads to a re-description of the text.

A deconstructive reading could, for example, focus on selected interview passages and phrases and work out the meanings expressed, as well as meanings concealed and excluded by the terms chosen. Rather than deconstructing an interview text, I shall here attempt to deconstruct a phrase recurrently evoked in interview literature, also in my own earlier writings – *'the interview dialogue'*.

We may start by wondering why the two similar terms 'interview' and 'dialogue' are often added together, and not uncommonly bolstered with embellishing words, such as 'authentic', 'real', 'genuine', 'egalitarian' and 'trusting'. When 'dialogue' is used in current interview research it is seldom in the severe Socratic form, but more commonly as warm caring dialogues. 'Dialogue' exists in a binary opposition to 'monologue', which today may connote an old-fashioned, authoritarian form of communication. 'Dialogical interviewing' can imply a warm empathetic caring, in contrast to alienated and objectifying forms of social research, such as experiments and questionnaires. When the interview is conceived as a dialogue, the researcher and the subject are then implied as egalitarian partners in a close mutually beneficial personal relation. The expression 'interview dialogue' here glosses over the asymmetrical power relationships of the interview interaction, where the interviewer initiates and terminates the interview, poses the questions, and usually retains a monopoly of interpreting the meaning of what the interviewer says (see Box 2.2).

We further note that the term 'dialogue' is used today in texts from a variety of fields such as management and education, when advocating 'dialogue between managers and workers' and 'dialogical education' (Kvale, 2006). In these contexts, with obvious power differences and often conflicts, the term 'dialogue' may provide an impression of equality and harmonious consensus. We shall conclude this brief deconstruction of the phrase 'interview dialogue' by asking whether the term 'dialogical interviews' used about research interviews may, corresponding to dialogical management and dialogical education, serve to embellish the power asymmetry and cover up potential conflicts of research interviewers and their interviewees.

Implications for interviewing As any kind of text may be made a subject of deconstruction, there are no specific requirements for interviewing. If a deconstruction of interview texts is considered, the interviewer may, however, address the use of key terms in a variety of contexts, from a multiplicity of perspectives, thereby providing a multi-faceted material for deconstruction.

Interview analysis as bricolage

Many analyses of interviews are conducted without following any specific analytic method. The researchers may then freely change between different techniques and approaches. Bricolage refers to mixed technical discourses where the interpreter moves freely between different analytic techniques. This eclectic form of generating meaning – through a multiplicity of ad hoc methods and conceptual approaches – is a common mode of interview analysis. In contrast to systematic analytic modes such as categorization and conversation analysis, bricolage implies a free interplay of techniques during the analysis. The researcher may here read the interviews through and get an overall impression, then go back to specific interesting passages, perhaps count statements indicating different attitudes to a phenomenon, cast parts of the interview into a narrative, work out metaphors to capture key understandings, attempt to visualize findings in flow diagrams, and so on. Such tactics of meaning generation may, for interviews lacking an overall sense at the first reading, bring out connections and structures significant to a research project. The outcome of this form of meaning generation can be in words, in numbers, in figures and flow charts, and in a combination of these.

Box 9.2   Ad hoc techniques of interview analysis

Noting patterns, themes (1), *seeing plausibility* (2) and *clustering* (3) help the analyst see 'what goes with what'. *Making metaphors* (4), like the preceding three tactics, is a way to achieve more integration among diverse pieces of data. *Counting* (5) is also a familiar way to see 'what's there'.

Making contrasts/comparisons (6) is a pervasive tactic that sharpens understanding. Differentiation sometimes is needed, too, as in *partitioning variables* (7).

We also need tactics for seeing things and their relationships more abstractly. These include *subsuming particulars under the general* (8); *factoring* (9), an analogue to a familiar quantitative technique; *noting relations between variables* (10); and *finding intervening variables* (11).

Finally, how can we systematically assemble a *coherent understanding* of data? The tactics discussed are *building a logical chain of evidence* (12) and *making conceptual/theoretical coherence* (13).

Source: Miles and Huberman (1994, pp. 245–6).

In line with a bricolage approach, Box 9.2 presents some useful ad hoc tactics for generating meaning in qualitative texts, arranged roughly from the descriptive to the explanatory, and from the concrete to the more conceptual and abstract. The box brings a summary from the book *Qualitative Data Analysis* by Miles and Huberman (1994), who also outline a variety of analytic techniques. To take one example, metaphor means to understand one kind of thing by means of another, thereby highlighting perhaps new aspects of a kind. A metaphor does not entail a definite conceptual structure to which a statement may be unequivocally categorized as belonging or not belonging. In the present text, 'making metaphors', such as the miner and the traveller, seeks to achieve more integration among the diverse conceptions of interview research by portraying and contrasting different understandings of interview knowledge.

In my grade study a bricolage of mixed methods was applied to pursue a connection between talkativity and grades, postulated by a pupil (Chapter 1). According to a questionnaire follow-up (Table 4.1), 82 percent of the pupils believed that high grades were often a question of how much one talks in class. When reading through the 30 pupils' interviews I had been struck by how significantly they varied in length, even though one school hour had been set aside for each interview. Following a hunch, I ranked the interviews according to number of pages, and then correlated the page numbers with the pupils' grade point averages. The resulting correlation was 0.65, with a chance probability of $p < 0.001$. There is thus a statistically significant connection between how much the pupils talked during the interviews and their grade point averages. The correlation is open to several interpretations: Do the pupils get high grades because they generally talk a great deal? Or are pupils who get high grades more reflected about grading, and more at ease with talking at length with an interviewer about grades?

This example demonstrates how it is possible to use a variety of techniques to investigate a hypothesis of a connection between grades and talkativity: by discussing the truth value of a pupil's interview statement in the interview itself, testing the generality of the belief in a questionnaire, and finding potential indirect statistical evidence in the length of interviews about grades. In this bricolage of mixed methods there is no epistemological primacy accorded to any of the methods and techniques, they are different means of investigating a provoking statement about grading.

Interview analysis as theoretical reading

A researcher may read through his or her interviews again and again, reflect theoretically on specific themes of interest, write out interpretation and not follow any systematic method or combination of techniques. We shall note that in several influential interview studies of the last few decades, leading to new knowledge in their discipline, no specific systematic analytic tools were used to analyse the interviews. This applies to the work of Bellah et al., Hargreaves, Bourdieu et al. and Sennett mentioned earlier. These investigations were based on an extensive and theoretically reflected knowledge of the subject matter, and in the studies by Bourdieu and Bellah also on a confronting Socratic interview form. No elaborate analytic techniques were applied at the theoretically reflected reading of the interviews to develop their rich meanings. This may perhaps suggest that recourse to specific analytic tools becomes less paramount with an extensive and theoretical knowledge of the subject matter of an investigation, and with a theoretically informed interview questioning.

In Hargreaves's study, *'Changing Teachers, Changing Times* (1994), the interviews with 40 teachers and principals had generated almost 1,000 pages of transcripts, which were read and re-read in order to establish a close familiarity with the data. Summary reports of each interview were written according to the key themes. Themes appearing in the text were registered, classified and re-classified on the basis of an active search for confirming and disconfirming evidence in the interviews. Hargreaves interrogated the data in a consciously eclectic approach, drawing in different concepts and theories. He describes his analytic approach as listening to the teachers' voices telling about their work and comparing their descriptions with claims about their work from literature. 'Throughout the study, I have attempted to sustain a creative dialogue between different theories and the data, in a quest not to validate any presumed perspective, but simply to understand the problems in their social context, as experienced by teachers' (Hargreaves, 1994, p. 122).

No tables or quantified categorizations of themes are presented in the book. The findings are reported in a continuous interpretative text, with interview passages interspersed, such as the sequence leading to the concept of 'contrived collegiality' (Box 1.2), which appeared unexpectedly from reading of the transcripts; 'In contrived collegiality, collaboration among teachers was compulsory, not voluntary; bounded and fixed in time and space; implementation- rather than development-oriented; and meant to be predictable rather than unpredictable in its outcomes' (Hargreaves, 1994, p. 208). In the book, interview passages are integrated in theoretically informed reflections on teacher work, drawing on management literature and postmodern analysis of culture. The results are striking descriptions of the Canadian teachers' work situation in a postmodern culture, in particular regarding increasing pressures on time and collegiality, descriptions that are well recognizable for teachers in Denmark.

Bourdieu et al. (1999) give little explicit textual interpretation of their interviews in *The Weight of the World*. Although elsewhere writing extensively and theoretically on the situation of the downtrodden in France, in this book Bourdieu mainly lets the many interviews reproduced in the text speak for themselves. However, the reader is aided in several ways. In an Appendix to the book – 'Understanding' – the approach to interviewing is described:

> ... it seems to me imperative to make explicit the intentions and procedural principles that we have put into practice in the research project whose findings we present here. The reader will thus be able to reproduce in the reading of the texts the work of both construction and understanding that produced them. (Bourdieu et al., 1999, p. 607)

When it is possible to let the interviews speak for themselves to a large extent, this may be because the interviews are preceded by a presentation of the social situation of the interviewees, allowing the reader to interpret their statements in relation to their life situation. Further, much of the analysis was already built into the interviews through a Socratic maieutic method of aiding explanations, such as formulating suggestions for open-ended continuations of interviewee statements, leading to an induced and accompanied self-analysis. Bourdieu also presents some key themes and analyses from an interview, such as the emotional impact upon himself of the interview with the two young men (Box 1.3):

> I did not have to force myself to share in the feeling, inscribed in every word, every sentence, and more especially in the tone of their voices, their facial expressions or body languages, of the *obviousness* of this form of collective bad luck that attaches itself, like a fate, to all those that have been put together in those sites of *social relegation*, where the personal suffering of each is augmented by all the suffering that comes from coexisting and living with so many suffering people together – and,

perhaps more importantly, of the destiny effect from belonging to a stigmatized group. (Bourdieu et al., 1999, p. 64)

▤ Key points

- The analysis of the interviews should be given thought from the beginning of an interview inquiry. The analysis starts when thematizing and designing the study, and the modes of analysis ought to be taken into account during the interviewing and transcription.
- The more the analysis is undertaken in the early stages of an interview investigation, the easier and the more qualified the later analysis will be.
- Interview analyses focusing on meaning include meaning condensation, meaning categorization and meaning interpretation.
- Interview analyses focusing on language include linguistic analysis, conversation analysis, narrative analysis, discursive analysis and deconstruction.
- Analysis as bricolage and as theoretical reflection goes beyond following specific techniques or approaches to interview analysis and draws in a variety of techniques and theoretical concepts.

Further reading

The following books will help you to go deeper into issues of analyzing interviews:

Gibbs, G.R. (2007) *Analyzing Qualitative Data* (Book 6 of *The SAGE Qualitative Research Kit*). London: Sage.

Miles, M.B. and Huberman, A.M. (1994) *Qualitative Data Analysis*. Thousand Oaks, CA: Sage.

Mishler, E.G. (1986) *Research Interviewing – Context and Narrative*. Cambridge, MA: Harvard University Press.

Potter, J. and Wetherell, M. (1987) *Discourse and Social Psychology*. London: Sage.

Rapley, T. (2007) *Doing Conversation, Discourse and Document Analysis* (Book 7 of *The SAGE Qualitative Research Kit*). London: Sage.

Silverman, D. (2006) *Interpreting Qualitative Data* (3rd ed.). London: Sage.

Tesch, R. (1990) *Qualitative Research: Analysis Types and Software Tools*. London: Falmer.

10
Validation and generalization of interview knowledge

Objectivity of interview knowledge   120
Reliability and validity of interview knowledge   122
Validity as quality of craftsmanship   123
Communicative and pragmatic validity   124
Generalizing from interview studies   *126*

Chapter objectives
After reading this chapter, you should know about

- implications for interview research of concepts of reliability, validity and generalization, which are commonly used for discussing issues of trustworthiness, strength and transferability of knowledge in the social sciences;
- discussions of objectivity of interview knowledge;
- reliability and validity in relation to the quality of craftsmanship throughout an entire interview inquiry;
- validation of the knowledge produced in an interview as a communicative and a pragmatic activity; and
- analytical generalization from interview studies.

Objectivity of interview knowledge

Issues of reliability and validity go beyond technical or conceptual concerns and raise epistemological questions of objectivity of knowledge and the nature of interview research. Objectivity is a rather ambiguous term, and I shall here distinguish between objectivity as freedom from bias, as intersubjective consensus, as adequacy to the object and as the object's ability to object.

Objectivity as *freedom from bias* refers to reliable knowledge, checked and controlled, undistorted by personal bias and prejudice. Such a commonsense conception of objective as being free of bias implies doing good, solid, crafts-man-like research, producing knowledge that has been systematically cross-checked and verified. In principle, a well-crafted interview can be an objective research method in the sense of being unbiased.

A conception of objective as meaning *intersubjective* knowledge has been common in the social sciences. With objectivity as intersubjective agreement we may distinguish between an arithmetical and a dialogical conception of objectivity. *Arithmetic intersubjectivity* refers to reliability as measured statistically by the amount of agreement among independent observers or coders. Interview analyses may in principle be objective in the sense of intersubjective agreement, such as when a high degree of intersubjective reliability is documented by cod-ing interviews in quantifiable categories.

Dialogical intersubjectivity refers to agreement through a rational discourse and reciprocal criticism between those interpreting a phenomenon. This may take the form of a communicative validation among researchers as well as between researchers and their subjects. Taking into account the power asymmetry of researcher and subjects, the interview attains a privileged position regarding objectivity as dialogical subjectivity – the interview is a conversation and a nego-tiation of meaning between the researcher and his or her subjects.

Objective may also mean reflecting the nature of the object researched, letting the object speak, being *adequate to the object* investigated, expressing the real nature of the object studied. Thus, if one conceives of the human world as basi-cally existing in numbers, a restriction of the concept of validation to measure-ment follows naturally, as only quantitative methods reflect the real nature of the social objects investigated. However, with the object of the interview understood as existing in a linguistically constituted and interpersonally negotiated social world, the qualitative research interview obtains a privileged position in produc-ing objective knowledge of the social world. The interview is sensitive to and reflects the nature of the object investigated – a conversational human world; in the interview conversation the object speaks.

Objectivity may also stand for *allowing the object to object*. Latour (2000) has suggested that it is by allowing the objects investigated to object to the natural sci-entists' interventions that one obtains maximum objectivity. He argues that objec-tivity in social science is also obtained by allowing 'the objects to object'. If social scientists wanted to become objective, they should, as natural scientists do, seek the rare, extreme, situations where their objects have maximum possibilities of protesting against what the researchers say about them – where the objects are allowed to raise questions in their own terms and not in the researcher's terms, a researcher whose interests they need not share. As an example from the social sciences he points to how feminism today has contributed to making women recalcitrant against the social researchers' interview approaches. We may here note that, in contrast to questionnaires, in principle, qualitative interviews allow the subjects to object to the presuppositions of the researcher's questions and interpretations.

We may conclude that, contrary to common opinion, knowledge produced in interviews need not be subjective, but may, in principle, be an objective method with respect to key meanings of objectivity. We shall now turn to the more specific discussions of objectivity in relation to reliability and validity.

Reliability and validity of interview knowledge

The concepts of reliability and validity are regarded by some qualitative researchers as being too laden with positivist conceptions from quantitative research and have been substituted with terms from common language, such as credibility, trustworthiness and the like. I shall here retain the traditional concepts of reliability and validity, which are also terms in the common language – as reflected in statements such as 'Is he reliable?', 'Your passport is not valid' or 'Your argument is not valid'. I shall reinterpret these concepts in ways appropriate to the construction of knowledge in interviews. With the varieties of interviewing and interview analysis (Chapters 6 and 9), and the differing epistemological conceptions of knowledge involved (Chapter 2), no general criteria for verification of the interview knowledge are suggested here. Thus, interviewing witnesses for factual knowledge raises other issues of validation than discursive analyses of interview interaction.

Reliability pertains to the consistency and trustworthiness of research findings; it is often treated in relation to the issue of whether a finding is reproducible at other times and by other researchers. This concerns whether the interview subjects will change their answers during an interview and whether they will give different replies to different interviewers. Issues of reliability also arise in connection with transcription and analysis of interviews, pertaining to whether different transcribers and analyzers will come up with similar transcriptions and analyses.

Validity refers in ordinary language to the truth, the correctness and the strength of a statement. A valid argument is sound, well grounded, justifiable, strong and convincing. Validity in the social sciences pertains to the issue of whether a method investigates what it purports to investigate. In a positivist approach to social science, validity becomes restricted to measurement; for instance, 'Validity is often defined by asking the question: Are you measuring what you think you are measuring?' (Kerlinger, 1979, p. 138). Qualitative research is then invalid if it does not result in numbers. In a broader conception, validity pertains to the degree that a method investigates what it is intended to investigate, to 'the extent to which our observations indeed reflect the phenomena or variables of interest to us' (Pervin, 1984, p. 48). With this open conception of validity, qualitative research can, in principle, lead to valid scientific knowledge.

When giving up the belief in one true objective social reality, the quest for absolute, certain knowledge, corresponding to an objective outer or essential inner reality, is replaced by a concern for the quality of the knowledge produced with an emphasis on defensible knowledge claims. Validation becomes the issue of choosing among competing and falsifiable interpretations, of examining and providing arguments for the relative credibility of alternative knowledge claims. Rather than proposing fixed validity criteria, three general approaches for validating interview knowledge will be suggested. They focus on the quality of the craftsmanship of the interview researcher, on the communication of interview findings and on their pragmatic effects.

Validity as quality of craftsmanship

Validation rests on the quality of the researcher's craftsmanship throughout an investigation, continually checking, questioning and theoretically interpreting the findings. Although treated in a separate chapter here, validation does not belong to a separate stage of an investigation, but permeates the entire research process. We are here moving the emphasis from a final product validation to a continual process validation. Interview craftsmanship involves addressing validity throughout the seven stages of an interview inquiry. I shall here discuss validation as checking, questioning and theorizing throughout an interview investigation.

To validate is to check
Validity is ascertained by examining the sources of invalidity. The stronger the falsification attempts a knowledge proposition has survived, the stronger and more valid is the knowledge. The researcher adopts a critical look at the analysis, presents his or her perspective on the subject matter studied and the controls applied to counter selective perceptions and biased interpretations. The interviewer here plays the devil's advocate towards his or her own findings.

In the grounded theory approach of Glaser and Strauss (1967), verification is built into the entire research process with continual checks on the credibility, plausibility and trustworthiness of the findings. Miles and Huberman (1994) approach validity by analyzing the many sources of potential biases that might invalidate qualitative observations and interpretations; they outline in detail tactics for testing and confirming qualitative findings, such as checking for representativeness and for researcher effects, triangulating, weighing the evidence, checking the meaning of outliers, using extreme cases, following up on surprises, looking for negative evidence, making if-then tests, ruling out spurious relations, replicating a finding, checking out rival explanations and getting feedback from informants.

To validate is to question

When ascertaining validity – that is, whether an investigation investigates what it seeks to investigate – the content and purpose of the study precede questions of method. The questions of 'what' and 'why' need to be answered before the question of 'how' to validate. Different questions regarding what and why posed to interview texts lead to different answers of how to validate an interpretation. Thus in the grading study, one type of research question led to an *experiential* reading of the pupils' statements about grades in high school, addressing the varieties of their individual experiences with grading. Another type of question led to a *veridical* reading, regarding the interviewees as witnesses or informants about the influence of grades on the social interaction in their class. The questioning also involved a *symptomatic* reading, focusing on the interviewees themselves and their individual reasons for making a given statement. Validation here differs with different questions posed to the interview texts.

To validate is to theorize

Validity is not only an issue of method. Ascertaining whether a method investigates what it intends to investigate involves a theoretical conception of what is investigated. In the terms of grounded theory, verifying interpretations is an intrinsic part of the generation of theory. Pursuing the methodological issues of validation generates theoretical and epistemological questions about the nature of the phenomena investigated. When treating discourse analysis in Chapter 9, I argued that if subjects frequently change their statements about their attitudes to, for example, immigrants during an interview, this is not necessarily due to an unreliable or invalid interview technique, but may in contrast testify to the sensitivity of the interview technique in capturing the multiple nuances and the fluidity of social attitudes.

Ideally, the quality of the craftsmanship in checking, questioning and theorizing the interview findings leads to knowledge claims that are so powerful and convincing in their own right that they, so to speak, carry the validation with them, like a strong piece of art. In such cases, the research procedures would be transparent and the results evident, and the conclusions of a study intrinsically convincing as true, beautiful and good. Appeals to external certification, or official validity stamps of approval, then become secondary, as validation is embedded in every stage of the construction of knowledge throughout an interview inquiry. In this sense, valid research would be research that makes questions of validity superfluous.

Communicative and pragmatic validity

When a modern belief in knowledge as a mirror of reality recedes to a social construction of social reality, communicative and pragmatic forms of validation

TABLE 10.1 Contexts of interpretation and communities of validation

Context of interpretation	Community of validation	Form of validation
Self-understanding	The interviewee	Member validation
Critical commonsense understanding	The general public	Audience validation
Theoretical understanding	The research community	Peer validation

come to the foreground. Method as a guarantee of truth dissolves; with a social construction of reality the discourse of the community becomes focal. Communication of knowledge becomes significant, with aesthetics and rhetoric entering into a scientific discourse.

Communicative validity involves testing the validity of knowledge claims in a conversation. What is a valid observation or interpretation is ascertained in a discourse of the appropriate community. A communicative validation of interview findings raises specific questions about the how, why and who of communication.

The three forms of communicative validation in Table 10.1 implicate different participants in a community of validation (see also Flick, 2007b). When the interviewer's interpretations refer to the subject's own understanding of their statements, the interviewee becomes the relevant partner for a conversation about the correct interpretation, involving what has been termed 'member validation'. The researcher's interpretations may also go beyond the subjects' self-understanding – what they themselves feel and think about a topic – while remaining within a critical commonsense understanding, such as in the case of the interpretation of the many denials of competition into a confirmation (Chapter 8) and with the deliberations of a jury on the trustworthiness of a witness. The general lay public is the relevant community of this 'audience validation'. In a third context, a theoretical frame for interpreting the meaning of a statement is applied. The interpretations are then likely to go beyond the interviewees' self-understanding and also to exceed a commonsense understanding, for example by an interpretation of grades as the currency of the educational system with a built-in contradiction of the use value and the exchange value of knowledge. In such cases, the relevant community of validation is scholars familiar with the interview themes and with the theories applied to the interview texts, and is referred to as 'peer validation'.

In the present perspective none of the three contexts provides more correct, authentic or deeper knowledge than the others; they are each appropriate to different research questions, which may be posed to interview statements. A communicative validation further raises power issues of how it is decided who is a competent and legitimate member of the interpretative community. The selection of members of the community to make decisions about issues of truth and value is considered decisive for the results in many cases, such as in the selection of members of a jury, and in a discipline of competing paradigms the composition of a committee to examine a doctoral candidate may be regarded as crucial.

Pragmatic validation relates to the users' responses to an interpretation, and in a strong form it concerns the issue of whether interventions based on the researcher's knowledge may instigate actual changes in behaviour. With a pragmatic movement from legitimation of knowledge to the use of knowledge, there is an emphasis on a pragmatic proof through action, and knowledge becomes the ability to perform effective actions. Criteria of efficiency and their desirability then become pivotal, raising ethical issues of right action. *Pragmatic validation* is verification in the literal sense – 'to make true'; justification is replaced by application. Knowledge is action rather than observation, the effectiveness of our knowledge beliefs is demonstrated by the effectiveness of our action.

Interview interpretations need not only be tested communicatively by direct questions, but also pragmatically by observations of the action consequences of the interviewer interpretations. Freud did not exclusively rely on the patient's self-understanding to validate therapeutic interpretations; taking neither a yes or a no for an answer, he recommended more indirect forms of validation, such as observing the patient's reactions to an interpretation, for example in the form of changes in the patient's free associations, dreams, recalling of forgotten memories, and alteration of neurotic symptoms (Freud, 1963, p. 279). Pragmatic validation also concerns reactions and collective actions in broader social settings; there are the reactions of a target audience to a system evaluation report, and the interaction of researcher and subjects in action research attempting to produce desired changes in a social system.

Generalizing from interview studies

If the findings of an interview study are judged to be reasonably reliable and valid, the question remains whether the results are primarily of local interest, or whether they may be transferable to other subjects and situations. A common objection to interview research is thus that there are too few subjects for the findings to be generalized.

A first reply to this objection is 'Why generalize?' Consistent demands for the social sciences to produce generalizable knowledge may involve an assumption of a universal knowledge valid for all places and times, for all humankind from eternity to eternity. In contrast, constructionist and discursive approaches conceive of social knowledge as socially and historically contextualized modes of understanding the social world. We may then ask, not whether an interview finding can be generalized globally, but whether the knowledge produced in a specific interview situation may be transferred to other relevant situations. The second reply to the above question is then 'How to generalize?' The answer is that interview-produced knowledge may be subjected to statistical as well as analytical forms of generalization.

Statistical generalization is formal and explicit. It is based on representative subjects selected at random from a population. Statistical generalization is feasible for interview studies using even a small number of subjects in so far as they are selected at random and the findings quantified (Chapter 4). However, due to the involved statistical presuppositions, the findings of a self-selected sample, such as volunteers for a treatment, cannot be transferred to the population at large.

Analytical generalization involves a reasoned judgement about the extent to which the findings from one study can be used as a guide to what might occur in another situation. We may here discern a researcher-based and a reader-based analytical generalization from interview studies. In the first case the researcher, in addition to rich specific descriptions, also offers arguments about the generality of his or her findings. In the latter case it is the reader who, on the basis of detailed contextual descriptions of an interview study, judges whether the findings may be generalized to a new situation.

In a discussion of the use of case studies in system evaluation, Kennedy (1979) argues for establishing rules for drawing inferences about the generality of qualitative findings from a case study, rules of inference that reasonable people can agree on. As models for inspiration, she turns to generalization in legal and clinical practice. In case law it is the most analogous preceding case, the one with the most attributes similar to the actual case, that is selected as the most relevant precedent. The validity of the generalization hinges on an analysis of the similarities and differences of the original and the present case, on the extent to which the attributes compared are relevant, which again presupposes rich, dense, detailed descriptions of the cases. Kennedy suggests criteria for relevant attributes of comparison in legal and clinical cases, that is, in the clinical situation the precision of description, longitudinal information and multidisciplinary assessment. It is the receiver of the information who determines the applicability of a finding to a new situation. In case law, the court decides whether a previous case offers a precedent that can be generalized to the case being tried: 'Like generalizations in law, clinical generalizations are the responsibility of the receiver of information rather than the original generator of information, and the evaluator must be careful to provide sufficient information to make such generalizations possible' (Kennedy, 1979, p. 672).

Analytical generalization and communicative validation both presuppose high-quality descriptions of the interview process and products. This points to the importance of how interview studies are reported, which is treated in the following chapter.

▤ Key points

- Common objections to interview studies concern their reliability, validity and generalization. While such criticisms are frequently based on criteria that may be adequate for quantitative research, alternative criteria may be appropriate for qualitative interview studies.
- Issues of validation are not confined to a separate stage of an interview inquiry, but permeate all stages from the first thematization to the final reporting.
- The validity of an interview will depend on the purpose of the interview and on epistemological conceptions of objectivity and knowledge.
- The validity of interview-produced knowledge rests on the quality of the craftsmanship of the interview researcher, continually checking, questioning and theorizing the interview findings.
- Validation may be conceived as a communicative activity, testing the findings of a study in a conversation.
- Validation may be regarded as pragmatic activity, testing the effectiveness of our knowledge by the effectiveness of our actions.
- Statistical generalization may be drawn from interview investigations with randomized sampling of subjects and quantification of the findings.
- Analytical generalization may be drawn from an interview investigation regardless of sampling and mode of analysis. Analytical generalization rests upon rich contextual descriptions. It includes the researcher's argumentation for the transferability of the interview findings to other subjects and situations, as well as the readers' generalizations from a report.

Further reading

Issues of validation and generalization in interview studies are addressed in some detail in these works:

Flick, U. (2007b) *Managing Quality in Qualitative Research* (Book 8 of *The SAGE Qualitative Research Kit*). London: Sage.

Kennedy, M.M. (1979) 'Generalizing from single case studies', *Evaluation Quarterly*, 3: 661–78.

Mishler, E.G. (1990) 'Validation in inquiry-guided research: the role of exemplars in narrative studies'. *Harvard Educational Review*, 60: 415–42.

Stake, R.E. (2005) 'Case studies', in N.K. Denzin and Y.S. Lincoln (eds), *Handbook of Qualitative Research*. Thousand Oaks, CA: Sage, pp. 443–66.

11
Reporting interview knowledge

Contrasting audiences for interview reports   129
Improving interview reports   130
Enhancing interview reports   133

Chapter objectives
After reading this chapter, you should know

- that the quality of an interview report attains a key position when validation and generalization of interview findings include communication with readers;
- about different audience reactions to interview reports;
- about ways of improving interview accounts methodologically; and
- about various ways of enhancing interview reports.

Contrasting audiences for interview reports

Throughout this book I have treated interviews and interview research as forms of conversation. The interview researcher has been depicted as a traveller in a foreign country, learning through his or her conversations with the inhabitants. When the traveller returns home with tales about encounters in the distant land, he or she may discover that local listeners react rather differently to these stories. At times it may be easier for interview researchers to carry out the conversations with their subjects than to enter into conversations with colleagues about their interview conversations.

When writing a report from an interview study it may be useful to be aware of different requirements within local social science communities. Authoritative requirements for a social science report may differ markedly across departments, disciplines, countries and epochs. In the discussion of interview quality, some mainstream objections to the objectivity of qualitative interview research were addressed (Box 7.5). Such objections are in line with a miner conception of interviewing as unearthing nuggets of data and meanings from the interview subjects. A contrasting audience consists of researchers in the qualitative field and the humanities, who may approach a postmodern understanding of the interviewer as a traveller returning home with tales from conversations in a distant country.

Before turning to improving and enhancing interview reports, some impressions of current interview reports will be mentioned. An interview situation may be experienced as exciting by the interview subjects and the interviewer, with continually new information, stories and insights turning up in their interaction. Reading the researcher's account from the interview stories may, however, be a tiresome undertaking in many cases. Through the analysis the subjects' originally exciting stories have been butchered into fragmented collections of long, obtuse, verbatim interview passages, with some scattered researcher comments. A fear of subjective interpretations may lead to reports that consist of an exasperating series of uninterpreted quotes, interspersed with paraphrasing of the quotes with hardly any new insights. The method steps of the interview journey may hardly be visible. Theoretical interpretations are often absent, as if they were some dangerous form of speculation.

Readers who find this description unduly negative are referred to Richardson and Adams St Pierre's more devastating criticism of current interview reports: 'I confessed that for years I had yawned my way through numerous supposedly exemplary of qualitative studies. Countless numbers of texts had I abandoned half read, half scanned. I would order a new book with great anticipation . . . only to find the text boring' (2005, p. 959). These authors emphasize the need to cultivate the writing skills of qualitative researchers and, inspired by postmodernism, suggest creative forms of writing, to the extent of treating 'writing as a method of inquiry'.

Improving interview reports

If readers find the results from an interview study of importance, they may want to know about the design and the methods that have produced this intriguing knowledge. In order to evaluate the quality, validity and transferability of the interview findings, information on the method steps of an investigation is required. In common interview reports the link between the original conversations and the conclusions reported may be thin or missing. The interested reader will not find any, or only come across some vague scattered descriptions of how the interview knowledge was produced. One may sometimes have the impression that an interview researcher has been so insecure about his or her method procedures that they are preferably left unmentioned. Rather than retaining a silence on method, the unique nature of a qualitative interview study poses a challenge to describe qualitatively as precisely as possible the method steps, procedures and decisions of the specific study.

Working towards the final report from the start of an interview study may contribute to a readable report of methodologically well-substantiated, interesting findings. The method steps from the original thematizing to the final report are then described in sufficient detail for the reader to ascertain the relevance of the interview design for the theme and purpose of the investigation, to evaluate the trustworthiness of the results, and, in principle, to be able to repeat the investigation.

Box 11.1 Investigating with the final report in mind

1. *Thematizing.* The earlier and clearer that interview researchers keep the end product of their study in sight – the story they want to tell – the easier the writing of the interview report will be.
2. *Designing.* Keep a systematic record of the design procedure as a basis for the method section of the final report. Have the final form of the interview report in mind when designing the study, including the ethical guidelines on informed consent with respect to later publication of the subjects' stories. With the ethical ideal that social research should serve to enhance the human situation, communicating research findings to the scientific and the general public is a key concern.
3. *Interviewing.* Ideally an interview is conducted in a form reportable to readers at the moment the tape recorder is turned off.
4. *Transcribing.* The readability of interviews that will be published should be kept in mind during transcription, as well as the protection of the subjects' confidentiality.
5. *Analysis.* In a narrative analysis, the analyzing and reporting of an interview merge and result in a story to be told to the readers. In other forms of analysis, too, the presentation of the results may be kept in mind, with the analysis of the interviews embedded in their reporting.
6. *Verification.* With an understanding of validation as communication and action, and with a conception of reader generalization, the quality of an interview report becomes a key concern.
7. *Reporting.* Working towards the final report from the start of an interview study should contribute to a readable report of methodologically well-substantiated and interesting findings.

Some of the information relevant to the final report about the research procedures throughout the seven stages of an interview investigation is shown in Box 11.1. Thus, pertinent information concerning the interview situation includes: What information was given to the subjects before the interview? What was the social and emotional atmosphere like, the degree of rapport during the interview? What kinds of questions were posed? How was the interview structured? Such information is important for interpreting the meaning of what was said in an interview.

The modes of presenting interview passages vary with the purpose of the investigation, ranging from precise verbatim quotes as done in conversation analysis to narrative restructuring. When presenting interview findings with the help of quotes, three guidelines for editing are suggested:

- *The quotes should be contextualized.* The quotations are fragments abstracted from an extensive interview context, which the interviewer knows well but which is unknown to the reader. It will be helpful to render the interview context of the quote, including the question that prompted an answer. The reader will then know whether a specific theme was introduced by the interviewer or by the subject, and also whether it was brought up in a way that led to a specific answer.

- *Interview quotes should be rendered in a readable style.* Interview excerpts in a vernacular form, in particular in local dialects, provide rough reading. Verbatim transcriptions of oral speech, with its characteristic repetitions, digressions, pauses, 'mms', and the like, are difficult to grasp when presented in a written form. The subject's spontaneous oral speech should, in order to facilitate comprehension, in the final report be rendered into a readable, written textual form. Exceptions to this are quotes for demonstration of linguistic and conversation analysis.

- *Interview quotes should preferably be loyal to the habitual language of an interviewee.* Some subjects may experience a shock when reading verbatim transcripts of their own interviews. Oral language transcribed verbatim may appear as incoherent and confused speech, even as indicating a lower level of intellectual functioning. The publication of incoherent and repetitive verbatim interview transcripts may involve an unethical stigmatization of the interviewees or the groups they belong to. They may become offended and refuse any further cooperation and use of what they have said. If the transcripts are to be sent back to the interviewees for member checks, rendering them in a more fluent written style might be considered from the start. And if not, consider accompanying the transcripts with information about the natural differences between oral and written language styles. One possible guideline for editing interview transcripts for a written report, doing justice to the interviewees, is to imagine how they themselves would have wanted to formulate their statements in writing. The transcriber then on behalf of the subjects seeks to translate their oral style into a written form in harmony with their habitual modes of expression.

Enhancing interview reports

Going beyond standard requirements for scientific reports, I shall suggest ways of enhancing the readability of interview accounts, taking leads from journalistic interviews, philosophical dialogues, case stories and narratives.

One form of reporting interviews is simply to present them as *interviews*. The social science researcher may here learn from journalists, who from the start of an interview will have a specific audience in mind and usually also a limited amount of space and a non-negotiable deadline. The newspaper or radio reporter can try to build the situation and the interpretations into the interview itself. The local context and social situation may be introduced through the interviewer's questions, for instance: 'We are now sitting in the living room of the house you built when you retired, with a view through the birch forest to the fjord. Could you tell me about … ?' The main points and interpretations may develop from the subject's replies to the journalist's questions, or be suggested by the journalist for confirmation or disconfirmation by the subject. Thus the contextualization and interpretation can be built into the conversation, with both journalist and interviewee more or less having the intended audience in mind. The guiding line throughout the interview, the transcribing and the editing will be to assist interviewed subjects to tell their stories as eloquently as possible to an anticipated audience.

A free and reflective approach to conversations and narratives is found in clinical *case stories*. Freud's case reports are one illustration of an engaging and artistic presentation of conversations, which are read and debated a century later.

Whereas case stories may contain reports of spontaneous or reconstructed stories, in a *narrative* approach interviewers may systematically conceive of their inquiry as storytelling from beginning to end. The report may then be a narrative rendering of subjects' spontaneous stories (compare the craftman's narrative in Box 6.2), or their stories as structured into specific narrative modes, or are recast into new stories by the researcher.

Interview findings may be represented in the form of the researcher's dialogue with the interview texts. Hargreaves's (1994) report of his interviews with school teachers consists of theoretical and conceptual discussions of literature confronted with interview statements from the teachers confirming, disconfirming or refining the understanding of teacher work in the existing literature. The continual theoretical questioning and elaboration of the teachers' statements allow for interesting reading.

Interviews can also be reported in the form of *dialogues*. Again, the information is conveyed by the interview interaction, but formalized and stylistically edited. In Socrates' conversations with his philosophical opponents, all of the information is included in the dialogue, without subsequent interpretations by the reporter – Plato. Independent of their historical status as verbatim reproductions or literary constructions, the content of Plato's dialogues continues to interest us today with the critical questions they pose as to the nature of truth, goodness and beauty.

Bourdieu et al. reported their interviews extensively, with key phrases from the interviews interspersed as subheadings:

> ... the kind of redaction proposed here: breaking with the spontaneous illusion of a discourse that 'speaks for itself', it deliberately *works off the* pragmatics of writing (particularly by adding headings and subheadings taken from phrases in the interview itself) to orient the reader's attention toward sociologically pertinent features which might escape unwary or distracted perception. (1999, pp. 621–2)

I shall conclude by an interview report breaking new ground: *Troubling the Angels – Women Living with HIV/AIDS* (Lather and Smithies, 1997). The researchers talked with HIV-positive women, in their support groups and individually, charting the journey of their struggles from infection to symptom, to sickness, to wasting, to death. The book is organized as layers of various kinds of information, where the major part is conversations in support groups for the women, with the researchers entering with questions and comments at times. The women's stories are interspersed with inter-texts on angels, chronicling the social and cultural issues raised by the disease. Factual information on HIV/AIDS is presented in boxes throughout the text. Across the bottom of much of the book is a running commentary by the co-researchers, moving between research methods and theoretical frameworks to the co-researchers' autobiographies throughout the inquiry, with their reactions to the research theme, such as the feelings of one researcher when waiting for and receiving her own HIV test.

The authors hoped with the book to provide support and information to the women and their friends and families and to promote public awareness of their issues. They had promised the women to be the editorial board for their book and prepared a desk copy version for the women's member checks. They participated eagerly in the process and could be frank with their impatience: 'Where is the book? Some of us are on the deadline, you know!' Challenging any easy reading via shifting styles and multiplication of layers of meaning, the final book attempts to do justice to the women's lives, positioning the reader as thinking, willing to trouble the taking-for-granted, opening to that which is beyond the word and the rational.

≡ Key points

- Interview reports may provide tiresome reading of a fragmented rendering of interview quotes. Modes of improving and enhancing interview reports are suggested, including learning from other genres such as journalistic interviews, philosophical dialogues, case stories and narratives.
- In order to ascertain the trustworthiness and the scope of the interview findings, the reader needs to know by which specific procedures the researcher obtained these results. The researcher may here strive towards a transparency of method procedures.
- In particular for communicative validation and analytical generalization, readers need rich contextual information about the interview findings in order to validate and generalize the results.

Further reading

Writing and reporting findings from interview studies are addressed in the following two publications:

Richardson, L. and Adams St Pierre, E. (2005) 'Writing: a method of inquiry', in N.K. Denzin and Y.S. Lincoln (eds), *Handbook of Qualitative Research*. Thousand Oaks, CA: Sage, pp. 959–78.
van Maanen, J. (1988) *Tales from the Field*. Chicago: Chicago University Press.

12
Enhancing interview quality

Learning the craft of interviewing   137
Value of interview knowledge   140
Epistemological and ethical conceptions of
interview knowledge   142

One thing is a chart to understand
Navigating a ship is something else
From a book on politics one may learn to reason
To rule a country, however,
More is required.

Ludvig Holberg (2004) *The Politicion Tinker*

Chapter objectives
After reading this chapter you should know

- after the draft of an interview journey this book has provided, that carrying out an interview inquiry is something else, and that more is required;
- what could be learned from the transcription task presented in the introduction;
- how a practicum for learning the craft of interviewing can be designed;
- that beyond the practical skills of the trade, reflections on the quality and the value of the knowledge produced by interviews are necessary;
- what to learn from reflecting internal criticisms of the value of current interview research; and
- about epistemological conceptions of knowledge valid to the conversational practice of producing knowledge through interviews.

Learning the craft of interviewing

Writing a book on the craft of interviewing involves a paradox of presenting explicit and general guidelines for a craft, which consists of practical skills and personal know-how that often remains tacit and depends on a given situation. While one does not become a good interviewer through reading a book about interviewing, a book can nevertheless provide some information about the terrain through which an interview journey goes, and about available equipment for the journey, and thereby facilitate the journey and enhance the quality of the knowledge that the interview traveller brings home. The preceding chapters have sought to present some of the multitude of courses that may be followed in an interview inquiry, outlining choices available and their consequences for the knowledge produced.

Box 12.1   Learning interviewing by transcribing interviews

Obtain about three tape-recorded research interviews, spend a week transcribing them, and reflecting on the processes and problems of transcribing and interviewing.

Learning lessons:

- To secure a good quality of the sound recording.
- To clarify inaudible answers during the interview.
- To pose clear questions that the interview subjects understand.
- To listen carefully to what is said and how it is said.
- To pay attention to the voice, the pauses, the sighs and the like, as indications that a topic may be important, and possibly also too sensitive to pursue.
- To follow up an interview statement by second questions.
- To avoid the interview becoming filled with small talk.
- To notice the interviewer variations of questioning styles, their advantages and their drawbacks.
- To become aware of the differences between oral and written language, and the need for guidelines for translation from oral to written language.
- To notice how new interpretations of the meanings may spontaneously arise when working closely with the oral recording.
- To become sensitive to the possible ethical transgressions by questioning too privately or critically.

At the start of this book I suggested that readers who wanted to learn interviewing in ways approximating the learning of a craft, should stop reading and perform the task described in Box 12.1 before continuing to read the book.

During a week of transcribing, newcomers to research interviewing will have discovered by themselves much of what has been spelled out in the previous chapters about interviewing and transcribing, some of which is spelled out as learning lessons in the box. The transcription task is inspired by Tilley's (2003) article 'Transcription work: learning through co-participation in research practices'.

Starting to learn interviewing by listening to tapes will sensitize novice interviewers to the oral medium of the interview craft. Learning interviewing by transcribing interviews promotes a discovery learning where, through their own practice, newcomers to the trade discover techniques and dilemmas of transferring live conversations to written texts. In a safe transcribing situation, the novice may become aware of the subtleties of interviewing, where he or she will not ruin the knowledge production of an important interview or ethically transgress the interviewees' borders in a live interview situation.

Learning the craft of interviewing is ideally done through apprenticeships within a research community. Not every novice interviewer will have access to a research group where interviewing is part of the daily practice. Or the researchers may not have time available for instructing novices. One option in the latter case could be, as with apprenticeship learning of the crafts, that the novice 'pays for the tuition' by performing the simple tasks necessary for the ongoing research project, such as transcribing and learning on the way. In the analysis stage there may also be a need for several coders of the transcripts, allowing the learner to work his way into the trade by performing the tasks of the trade. In lieu of such an active qualitative interview research community, there are possibilities of self-study; inspired by Schön's (1987) practicum for educating the reflecting practitioner, I shall outline an interview practicum for learners at different stages of mastering the craft of interviewing.

Box 12.2 An interview practicum

- *I. Learn interviewing by witnessing others interviewing.*
  Sit in with a more experienced researcher who is interviewing, listen and observe, and gradually become active, take care of the recording and participate as a co-interviewer.
  Learning lessons:
  - Differences between the live interview situation and the tape-recorded speech.
  - Significance of the social relationship of interviewer and interviewee.
  - Importance of interviewers being knowledgeable of the topics they are asking about.
  - Value of staging and scripting an interview in advance.

  (Continued)

(Continued)

- *II. Learn interviewing by practising interviewing.*
  Learning lessons:
  - Acquiring self-confidence through gradual mastery of the practical, technical, social and conceptual issues of interviewing, and thereby becoming able to create a safe and stimulating interview situation.
  - Options for improving the content, formulation and sequence of the questions.
  - Become aware of the importance of mastering the art of second questions.
  - Videotaping some pilot interviews will heighten sensitivity to the body language of interviewer and interviewee.

- *III. Learn interviewing in a community of interview researchers.*
  Learning occasions:
  - With several interviewers working at different stages of their projects an impression is obtained of the overall designing of an interview inquiry.
  - Listening to interviews and interviewer stories about interviews.
  - Receiving feedback on one's own pilot interviews from more experienced interviewers.
  - Have another researcher interview you about your research theme, and uncover unreflected assumptions and personal biases to your interview theme.

Some of the learning occasions in an interview practicum with other newcomers and in a regular research group are listed in Box 12.2, with some of the lessons to be learned, summed up from the preceding chapters of this book. The transcription task and the interview practicum have focused on two of the seven stages of an interview inquiry – transcribing and interviewing. In corresponding ways the other stages of an interview inquiry may be learned in an interview practicum or in a research community, which provides a possibility to observe and, to some extent, also assist more experienced performers of the trade. Also an extensive study of interviews made by masters of the trade can support acquiring the skills of the trade, such as by reading the clinical interviews in Rogers's *Client-Centered Therapy* (1956) and the research interviews in Bourdieu et al.'s *The Weight of the World – Social Suffering in Contemporary Society* (1999).

The road to mastery of interviewing through a transcribing task, an interview practicum, or ideally a research apprenticeship, may appear as too cumbersome and time-consuming to some students. Rather than such a slow learning process they may prefer fast learning in a crash course in interview techniques and then go straight on with their own interview project. In this respect we should keep in mind that therapeutic interviewers, as well as commercial interviewers, who live by the value of their interview findings to their employers, may require several years of training to master the craft of interviewing (Chapter 4). While this may not be realistic in a crammed university program, the time needed for developing professional interviewing skills should not be overlooked in academic interview research.

Value of interview knowledge

Learning interview research goes beyond a technical mastery of the interview craft to include professional reflection on interview practice and on the value of the interview-produced knowledge, with an awareness of the epistemological and ethical issues involved. Interview research may be controversial, and different audiences may judge the value of an interview inquiry rather differently. Some well-established mainstream objections to interview research, close to a miner approach to interviewing, were presented in Box 7.5. Today dissatisfaction in a different vein comes from audiences sympathetic to the idea of qualitative interview research, such as scholars in the humanities and professionals like therapists. These critics are closer to an understanding of the interviewer as a traveller returning home with tales from conversations in a new country.

Box 12.3 Internal criticisms of interview research

Current interview research is:

- *Individualistic* – it focuses on the individual and neglects a person's embeddedness in social interactions.
- *Idealistic* – it ignores the situatedness of human experience and behaviour in a social, historical and material world.
- *Credulous* – it takes everything an interviewee says at face value, without maintaining a critical attitude.
- *Intellectualistic* – it neglects the emotional aspects of knowledge, overlooks empathy as a mode of knowing.
- *Cognitivist* – it focuses on thoughts and experiences at the expense of action.
- *Immobile* – the subjects sit and talk, they do not move or act in the world.
- *Verbalizing* – it makes a fetish of verbal interaction and transcripts, neglects the bodily interaction in the interview situation.
- *A-linguistic* – although the medium is language, linguistic approaches to language are absent.
- *A-theoretical* – it entails a cult of interview statements, and disregards theoretical analyses of the field studied.
- *A-rhetorical* – published reports are boring collections of interview quotes, rather than convincing stories.
- *Insignificant* – it produces trivialities and hardly any new knowledge worth mentioning.

Some of the insider objections to current interview research are presented in Box 12.3. Several of these objections can be addressed by methodological means. The individualist trend of interview research may thus be compensated by the social interaction of focus group interviews. The social embedding of the interviewees may be taken into account by accompanying field studies. The verbal fixation of interview research can be counteracted by videotaped interviews to a certain extent, thereby retaining access to bodily expressions and interpersonal dynamics. While most research interviews today are chair-bound, researchers might learn from radio and TV interviewers, who may walk around with their subjects in their natural surroundings, such as their workplace or home. Conversations integrated in the subjects' daily world can contribute to situating the interviewees' activities in a social and material world, and as action research potentially contribute to changing the social situation.

Alternative research approaches exist, more appropriate to several of the concerns about research interviews raised above. A comprehensive understanding of cultural situations is better acquired through field studies, which may also encompass more or less casual interviews. Knowledge about changing social activities may better be obtained in action research than merely by verbal interviews. Moreover, knowledge of a person's feelings and fantasies through intense emotional interaction is methodically and ethically accessible through intensive emotional interviews in long-term therapeutic relationships.

Regarding the last criticism of insignificant interview findings, the often boring reading of current interview reports, as discussed in the preceding chapter, may not only be a matter of the rhetorics of reporting, but may also concern the results of an interview study. There may occur a lack of substantial findings in some published interview reports, a lack of significant new knowledge in relation to existing commonsense or established scholarly knowledge. In contrast to the contributions of psychoanalytic interviews and sociological and ethnographic field studies, it is harder to point out significant new bodies of knowledge that have come from current qualitative interview research.

There exists a certain contrast between visions from the 1980s of a radically new research method in the social sciences and the amount of significant new knowledge produced today by qualitative interviews. Many textbooks on qualitative paradigms and methodology have appeared, but few breakthroughs in knowledge. The interview studies mentioned in this book by Bellah, Bourdieu, Hargreaves, Sennett and Schön, based on an extensive theoretical pre-knowledge of their interview themes, are exceptions to this. Furthermore, they remain – in contrast to current interview studies with often extensively paradigmatic legitimations of methodology – generally silent on the variety of qualitative paradigms, and bring rather short depictions of the methods used. The major emphasis remains on the interview findings and their theoretical and practical implications. Perhaps we encounter in current interview research a negative correlation between the number of pages on methodological paradigms and the number of pages contributing with substantial new knowledge in a field.

Epistemological and ethical conceptions of interview knowledge

Improving the quality of knowledge production in research interviews is not merely a question of improving the research skills of the individual researchers, or of enlarging the methodological scope of ways of interviewing. Enhancing interview quality is also a conceptual issue, which – beyond the theoretical knowledge of the subject matter of the investigation just mentioned – also entails an attention to epistemological and ethical issues raised by research conversations about private lives for public consumption.

Learning 'how' to produce interview knowledge of high quality presupposes adequate conceptions of the 'what' and 'why' of the interviewing – the nature of interview knowledge and the purpose of the interview inquiry. Faulty theoretical conceptions of interview conversations, such as the empiricist prejudice of leading questions, may lead to superficial interview practices.

Professional academic interview research includes reflecting on the theoretical issues of the research topic, as well as being aware of the ethical and epistemological assumptions involved in an interview study. Taking a position on these principal issues goes beyond learning through practising interviews to also encompass theoretical studies through books and academic seminars. Drawing on pragmatic and postmodern philosophy, I shall suggest conceptions of knowledge adequate to the nature of interview conversations. They may provide a frame of reference for reflection on, and directions for enhancing, the quality and value of interview research. They include the pragmatic, the situational, the linguistic and the conversational nature of interview knowledge.

Pragmatic knowledge

In the present book there has been a pragmatic emphasis on learning interviewing from practice, not only from one's own interview practice, but also from the practices of historical interview studies – studies that have led to significant differences in the way we understand social phenomena. This implies a move from interview research as methodological rule-following, with method as a truth guarantee, to research as craft, where craftsmanship is learned through practice, and with the value of the knowledge produced as the key quality criterion.

A pragmatic approach involves a move from philosophical legitimation to the practical effects of knowledge. Today we may discern a move from questions about objectivity and validity of interview knowledge to the quality and value of the knowledge produced. Rather than asking general paradigmatic questions such as 'Is the interview a scientific method?' or 'Is the knowledge from qualitative interviews objective?', pragmatic questions are more specific, such as 'Is this interview-produced knowledge useful?' 'And useful for whom and for what?' 'Are these results worthwhile, valuable, insightful and beneficial?' The question of application again raises the issue of useful and beneficial for what purposes and to whom, leading to ethical and socio-political questions about the use of the knowledge produced.

Situated knowledge

Interview knowledge is produced in a specific interpersonal situation, and the situational and interactional factors influencing the knowledge produced need to be taken into account, such as is done today in discursive and conversation analyses of interviews. Rather than seeking universal knowledge, the emphasis is on situated knowledge. What matters is not arriving at context-independent general knowledge, but producing well-described situated knowledge from the interviews. The transfer value of this knowledge to other situations may then be critically evaluated by other researchers and by lay readers.

Produced knowledge

In contrast to a miner metaphor of interviewing as collecting knowledge for later analysis by appropriate programs, the present approach goes beyond a prevalent separation of data collection and data analysis. Interview knowledge is not collected, but produced between interviewer and interviewee, and the meanings constructed in their interaction are again restructured throughout the later stages of an interview inquiry. There is an emphasis on knowledge production throughout the interview inquiry, such as enhancing the quality of the knowledge produced in the original interview situation, taking account of the constructive character of transcripts, as well as efforts to enrich the knowledge production by reporting the interviews to the readers.

Linguistic knowledge

In line with an understanding of interviews as a specific form of conversation, the skilled interviewer needs to master the medium of conversation – language. For a professional analysis of the language of the interviews and their transcripts, the researcher should be familiar with linguistic tools for analysis of language. Social scientists working with numbers as a rule employ professional tools for the analysis of numbers, such as statistics. In graduate social science programs, courses in statistics tend to be mandatory and courses in linguistics non-existent. In order to reach a professional level comparable to quantitative analysis today, qualitative social research needs to move beyond a linguistic illiteracy towards a professional mastery of the linguistic medium of the interview craft.

143

Conversational knowledge

We live in a conversational world. The relevance of conversations in social science goes beyond the use of interview conversations as an additional empirical method. It includes conversations among researchers, and the public, about the truth and value of the knowledge produced in interview conversations about a conversational world. In the neo-pragmatic philosophy of Richard Rorty the conversation thus has a primary role: 'If we see knowledge as a matter of conversation and social practice, rather than as an attempt to mirror nature ...', the conception of knowledge as re-presenting an objective world is discarded. We may then regard the ' ... *conversation* as the ultimate context within which knowledge is understood' (1979, pp. 171, 389). From an understanding of objectivity as letting the object speak, and object, the qualitative research interview obtains a privileged position for producing objective knowledge of a conversational world.

We exist in a conversational circle, where our understanding of the social world depends on conversations and our understanding of conversation is based on our understanding of the social world. This is not a vicious circle, but in a hermeneutical sense a *circulus fructuosis*. The problem is not to get out of the conversational circle but to get into it the right way. We may conceive this task as mastering a 'third-order hermeneutics'. The first hermeneutics consists of the interview subjects' understanding of their conversational activity, already existing. The interviewer then undertakes a second hermeneutical interpretation of the interviewees' first-order meanings as stated in the interview conversations. If the interviewer then returns his or her second-order interpretations to the interviewee, the interpretations may, through a third hermeneutical move, enter into and modify the subjects' first hermeneutical interpretation of their activities. And if the interviewer's interpretations are further reported in the public conversation, they may potentially change the public's understanding of themselves and their everyday world. This has happened with psychoanalytic interview interpretations, which, to a certain extent, have today become part of Western subjects' understanding of themselves.

Such public effects of interview research again draw in ethical conversations about whether the outcomes have been beneficial and to whom. One arena for raising such questions may be to follow the lead of Bellah and co-workers and to use interviews to enhance the public conversation. Interviews may, when critically carried out and well presented – such as the interview studies by Bellah et al. on individualism in the United States and by Bourdieu et al. on the plight of the downtrodden in France – incite the reader to enter the conversation and argue with what is said, stimulate a public opinion tested in the arena of public discussion.

Further reading

Issues of enhancing the quality of qualitative research and interviews are discussed in more detail in:

Flick, U. (2007a) *Designing Qualitative Research* (Book 1 of *The Sage Qualitative Research Kit*). London: Sage.

Flick, U. (2007b) *Managing Quality in Qualitative Research* (Book 8 of *The Sage Qualitative Research Kit*). London: Sage.

‖ Glossary

Audience validation The researcher's interpretations are here presented to a lay public for discussion of their validity.

Bricolage Refers to mixed technical and conceptual discourses where the interpreter moves freely between different analytic techniques and theories.

Categorization Involves a systematic coding of a statement into given categories allowing for quantification.

Coding Breaks a text down into manageable segments and attaches one or more keywords to a text segment in order to permit later retrieval of the segment.

Communicative validity Involves testing the validity of knowledge claims in a conversation.

Confidentiality Implies that private data identifying research subjects will not be reported.

Confrontational interview An interview where the interviewer actively confronts and challenges the views of the interviewee.

Conversation An oral exchange of observations, opinions and ideas.

Conversation analysis A meticulous method for studying talk in interaction. It is about what words and sentences do; the meaning of a statement is the role it plays in a specific social practice.

Craft An occupation requiring special skills and personal know-how, developed through training and long practice.

Deconstruction Involves destruction of one understanding of a text and opening for reconstruction of other understandings. The focus is not on what the person who uses a concept means, but on what the concept says and does not say in a text.

Discourse analysis Focuses on the interaction within discourses, on how the talk is constructed and what the power effects are of different discursive presentations of a topic. Related to conversation analysis, discourse analysis goes beyond a rigorous concentration on linguistic interaction to more broadly ranging interpretations.

Discursive interviewing An active form of interviewing focusing on the linguistic and social interaction in the interview situation.

Elite interviews Refer to interviews with persons who are leaders or experts in a community, people who are usually in powerful positions.

Epistemology The study of the nature of knowledge and justification.

Ethic of care An ethics that emphasizes empathy and compassion in personal relationships and a concern with the just community.

Ethic of duty A Kantian ethics of principles, which judges an action according to its intentions independently of consequences.

Focus group interview Refers to a group interview where a moderator seeks to focus the group discussion on specific themes of research interest.

Generalizability Refers to the extent that findings in one situation can be transferred to other situations.

Hermeneutics The study of interpretations of texts in the humanities. Hermeneutical interpretation seeks to arrive at valid interpretations of the meaning of a text. There is an emphasis on the multiplicity of meanings in a text, and on the interpreter's foreknowledge of the subject matter of a text.

Informed consent Entails informing the research subjects about the overall purpose and design of an investigation and obtaining their consent to participate.

Institutional review board (IRB) A board that reviews research proposals with respect to their compliance with ethical guidelines.

Interviewer questions Refer to the questions in everyday language that the interviewer poses to the interviewees.

Linguistic analysis Addresses the characteristic uses of language in an speech or text segment, such as the application of grammatical and linguistic forms, the implied speaker and listener positions and the use of metaphors.

Macro-ethics Concerns the value and effects of the research-produced knowledge in a socio-political context.

Meaning condensation Entails an abridgement of the meanings of an interviewee statement into shorter formulations, usually remaining within the understanding and language of the interviewee.

Meaning interpretation Goes beyond a structuring of the manifest meanings of what is said to deeper and critical interpretations of the text.

Member validation The researcher's interpretations are here presented to the subjects of an inquiry for discussion of their validity.

Method A systematic, more or less rule-based, procedure for observation and analysis of data.

Micro-ethics Concerns the social interaction in the research situation and the protection of the research subjects.

Mixed methods A term used today to refer to the combination of different kinds of methods in an investigation, sometimes raised in the form of paradigmatic contrasts of quantitative and qualitative methods.

Narrative analysis Focuses on the meaning and the linguistic form of texts, it works out plots of interview stories and temporal and social structures.

Narrative interviewing Interviewing to elicit or co-construct narratives in the interview, leading to a story with a distinct plot, a social interaction and a temporal unfolding.

Peer validation The researcher's interpretations are here presented to peers among researchers for discussion about their validity.

Phenomenology Rests upon careful descriptions and analyses of consciousness, with a focus on the subjects' life world. There is an attempt to bracket foreknowledge and a search for invariant essential meanings of the described phenomena.

Positivism A philosophy that bases science on the observation of data and where the observation of data should be separated from the interpretation of their meanings. Scientific knowledge is to be found by following general rules of method, largely independent of the content and context of the investigation.

Postmodernism A philosophy characterized by a disbelief in modern universal systems of knowledge. There is an emphasis on the conversational, the narrative, the linguistic, the contextual and the interrelational nature of knowledge.

Pragmatic validity Relates to the responses of the users of an interpretation; in a strong form it concerns whether interventions based on the researcher's interpretations may instigate actual changes in behaviour.

Pragmatism Involves a move from philosophical legitimation of knowledge to the practical effects of knowledge. Knowledge is justified through application; the strength of our knowledge beliefs is demonstrated by the effectiveness of our actions.

Reliability Pertains to the consistency and trustworthiness of a research account; intra- and inter-subjective reliability refer to whether a finding can be replicated at other times and by other researchers using the same method.

Research interview A conversation with a structure and a purpose; it involves careful questioning and listening with the purpose of obtaining thoroughly tested knowledge.

Research questions Refer to the researcher's conceptual and theoretical questions to the theme investigated.

Scripting Implies preparing an interview guide with suggestions for interview questions and their sequence.

Second questions Refer to on-the-spot questions following up an interviewee's answers.

Semi-structured life-world interview A planned and flexible interview with the purpose of obtaining descriptions of the life world of the interviewee with respect to interpreting the meaning of the described phenomena.

Staging Entails setting the stage for the interview through briefing and debriefing the subjects about the topic and purpose of the interview.

Thematizing Refers to the explicit formulation of the researcher's conceptualization of the subject matter and the purpose of an investigation.

Utilitarian ethics An ethics of consequences after Hume and Bentham, where an action is judged pragmatically by its effects.

Validity Pertains to the strength and soundness of a statement; in the social sciences, validity usually means whether a method investigates what it purports to investigate.

Virtue ethic An ethics of practical reasoning after Aristotle, where the personal integrity of the researcher and his or her interaction with the community is crucial.

III References

Adorno, T.W., Frenkel-Brunswik, E., Levinson, D.J. and Sanford, R.N. (1950) *The Authoritarian Personality*. New York: Norton.

American Psychological Association (1981) 'Ethical principles of psychologists', *American Psychologist,* 36: 633–8.

Angrosino, M. (2007) *Doing Ethnographic and Observational Research* (Book 3 of *The SAGE Qualitative Research Kit*). London: Sage.

Atkinson, P. and Silverman, D. (1997) 'Kundera's immortality: the interview society and the invention of the self', *Qualitative Inquiry*, 3: 304–25.

Banks, M. (2007) *Using Visual Data in Qualitative Research* (Book 5 of *The SAGE Qualitative Research Kit*). London: Sage.

Barbour, R. (2007) *Doing Focus Groups* (Book 4 of *The SAGE Qualitative Research Kit*). London: Sage.

Bellah, R.N., Madsen, R., Sullivan, W.M.S.A. and Tipton, S.M. (1985) *Habits of the Heart: Individualism and Commitment in American Life*. Berkeley: University of California Press.

Bornat, J. (2004) 'Oral history', in C. Seale, G. Gobo, J.F. Gubrium and D. Silverman, (eds), *Qualitative Research Practice*. London: Sage, pp. 34–47.

Bourdieu, P. et al. (1999) *The Weight of the World – Social Suffering in Contemporary Society*. Stanford, CA: Stanford University Press.

Brinkmann, S. and Kvale, S. (2005) 'Confronting the ethics of qualitative research', *Journal of Constructivist Psychology*, 18: 157–81.

Chrzanowska, J. (2002) *Interviewing Groups and Individuals in Qualitative Market Research*. Thousand Oaks, CA: Sage.

Denzin, N.K. and Lincoln, Y.S. (eds) (2005) *The Sage Handbook of Qualitative Research* (3rd ed.). Thousand Oaks, CA: Sage.

Dichter, E. (1960) *The Strategy of Desire*. Garden City, NY: Doubleday.

Duncombe, J. and Jessop, J. (2002) "Doing rapport" and the ethics of "faking friendship", in M. Mauthner, M. Birch, J. Jessop and T. Miller (eds), *Ethics in Qualitative Research*. London: Sage, pp. 107–22.

Eder, D. and Fingerson, L. (2002) 'Interviewing children and adolescents', in J.F. Gubrium, and J.A. Holstein (eds), *Handbook of Interview Research*. Thousand Oaks, CA: Sage, pp. 181–201.

Eisner, E.W. and Peshkin, A. (eds) (1990) *Qualitative Inquiry in Education*. New York: Teachers College Press.

Elster, J. (1980) 'Metode', in *PaxLeksikon*, Vol. 4. Oslo: Pax.

Fielding, N. (ed.) (2003) *Interviewing*, Vols. I–IV. Thousand Oaks, CA: Sage.

Fischer, C. and Wertz, F. (1979) 'Empirical phenomenological analyses of being criminally victimized', in A. Giorgi, R. Knowles and D.L. Smith (eds), *Duquesne Studies in Phenomenological Psychology, III*. Pittsburgh, PA: Duquesne University Press, pp. 135–58.

Flick, U. (2006) *An Introduction to Qualitative Research* (3rd ed.). Thousand Oaks, CA: Sage.

Flick, U. (2007a) *Designing Qualitative Research* (Book 1 of *The SAGE Qualitative Research Kit*). London: Sage.

Flick, U. (2007b) *Managing Quality in Qualitative Research* (Book 8 of *The SAGE Qualitative Research Kit*). London: Sage.

Fog, J. (2004). *Med samtalen som udgangspunkt* (*With the Conversation as Point of Departure*). Copenhagen: Akademisk Forlag.

Foucault, M. (1972). *The Archaeology of Knowledge*. New York: Pantheon.

Freud, S. (1963) *Therapy and Technique*. New York: Collier.

Gibbs, G.R. (2007) *Analyzing Qualitative Data*. (Book 6 of *The SAGE Qualitative Research Kit*). London: Sage.

Giorgi, A. (1975) 'An application of phenomenological method in psychology', in A. Giorgi, C. Fischer and E. Murray (eds), *Duquesne Studies in Phenomenological Psychology, II*. Pittsburgh, PA: Duquesne University Press, pp. 82–103.

Giorgi, A. and Giorgi, B. (2003) 'The descriptive phenomenological psychological method', in P. Camic, J. Rhodes and L. Yardley (eds), *Qualitative Research in Psychology: Expanding Perspectives in Methodology and Design*. Washington, DC: American Psychological Association Press, pp. 275–97.

Glaser, B.G. and Strauss, A.M. (1967) *The Discovery of Grounded Theory: Strategies for Qualitative Research*. New York: Aldine.

Gubrium, J.F. and Holstein, J.A. (eds) (2002) *Handbook of Interview Research*. Thousand Oaks, CA: Sage.

Guidelines for the Protection of Human Subjects. (1992). Berkeley: University of California Press.

Hargreaves, A. (1994) *Changing Teachers, Changing Times*. New York: Teachers College Press.

Hertz, R. and Imber, J.B. (eds) (1995) *Studying Elites Using Qualitative Methods*. Thousand Oaks, CA: Sage.

Holberg, L. (2004) *The Political Tinker*. Kila, MT: Kessinger.

Holstein, J.A. and Gubrium, J.F. (1995). *The Active Interview*. Thousand Oaks, CA: Sage.

Howe, R. (2004) 'A critique of experimentialism', *Qualitative Inquiry*, 10: 42–61.

Hvolbøl, C. and Kristensen, O.S. (1983) 'Bivirkninger ved karaktergivning' ('Side effects of grading'), *Psychological Reports Aarhus*, 8(1). Aarhus, Denmark: Aarhus Universitet.

Jensen, K.B. (1989) 'Discourses of interviewing: validating qualitative research findings through textual analysis', in S. Kvale (ed.), *Issues of Validity in Qualitative Research*. Lund, Sweden: Studentlitteratur, pp. 93–108.

Keats, D.M. (2000). *Interviewing – A Practical Guide for Students and Professionals*. Buckingham, UK: Open University Press.

Kennedy, M.M. (1979) 'Generalizing from single case studies', *Evaluation Quarterly*, 3: 661–78.

Kerlinger, F.N. (1979) *Behavioral Research*. New York: Holt, Rinehart & Winston.

Kimmel, A.J. (1988) *Ethics and Values in Applied Social Science Research*. Newbury Park, CA: Sage.

Kvale, S. (1972) *Prüfung und Herrschaft* (*Examination and Dominance*). Weinheim, Germany: Beltz.

Kvale, S. (1980) *Spillet om karakterer i gymnasiet – Elevinterviews om bivirkninger af adgangsbegrænsning* (*The Grading Game in High School – Interviews with Pupils about Side Effects of Grade-based Restricted Admissions*). Copenhagen: Munksgaard.

References

Kvale, S. (1996a) *InterViews – An Introduction to Qualitative Research Interviewing.* Thousand Oaks, CA: Sage.

Kvale, S. (1996b) 'Evaluation as construction of knowledge', in R. Hayhoe and J. Pan (eds), *East-West Dialogue Knowledge and Higher Education.* New York: Sharpe, pp. 117–40.

Kvale, S. (1997) 'Research apprenticeship', *Nordisk Pedagogik – Journal of Nordic Educational Research,* 17: 186–94.

Kvale, S. (2003) 'The psychoanalytic interview as inspiration for qualitative research', in P. Camic, J. Rhodes and L. Yardley (eds), *Qualitative Research in Psychology: Expanding Perspectives in Methodology and Design.* Washington, DC: American Psychological Association Press, pp. 275–97.

Kvale, S. (2006). 'Dominance through interviews and dialogues', *Qualitative Inquiry,* 12: 480–500.

Lather, P. and Smithies, C. (1997) *Troubling the Angels – Women Living with HIV/AIDS.* Boulder, CO: Westview Press.

Latour, B. (2000) 'When things strike back – a possible contribution of "science studies" to the social sciences', *British Journal of Sociology,* 51: 107–23.

Lave, J. and Kvale, S. (1995) 'What is anthropological research? An interview with Jean Lave by Steinar Kvale', *Qualitative Studies in Education,* 8: 219–28.

Lincoln, Y. (2005) 'Institutional review boards and methodological conservatism: the challenge to and from phenomenological paradigms', in N.K. Denzin and Y.S. Lincoln (eds), *The Sage Handbook of Qualitative Research.* (3rd ed.). Thousand Oaks, CA: Sage, pp. 165–81.

Loftus, E.L. and Palmer, J.C. (1974) 'Reconstruction of automobile destruction: an example of the interaction between language and memory', *Journal of Verbal Learning and Verbal Behavior,* 13: 585–9.

Lyotard, J.F. (1984) *The Postmodern Condition: A Report on Knowledge.* Manchester, UK: Manchester University Press.

Marshall, C. and Rossman, G.B. (2006) *Designing Qualitative Research* (4th ed.). Thousand Oaks, CA: Sage.

Mauthner, M., Birch, M., Jessop, J. and Miller, T. (eds) (2002) *Ethics in Qualitative Research.* Thousand Oaks, CA: Sage.

Memon, A. and Bull, R. (eds) (2000) *Handbook of the Psychology of Interviewing.* New York: Wiley.

Miles, M.B. and Huberman, A.M. (1994) *Qualitative Data Analysis.* Thousand Oaks, CA: Sage.

Mishler, E.G. (1986) *Research Interviewing – Context and Narrative.* Cambridge, MA: Harvard University Press.

Mishler, E.G. (1990) 'Validation in inquiry-guided research: the role of exemplars in narrative studies', *Harvard Educational Review,* 60: 415–42.

Mishler, E.G. (1991) 'Representing discourse: the rhetoric of transcription', *Journal of Narrative and Life History,* 1: 255–80.

Mishler, E.G. (1999) *Storylines – Craftartist's Narratives of Identity.* Cambridge, MA: Harvard University Press.

Ong, W.J. (1982) *Orality and Literacy – The Technologizing of the Word.* London: Methuen.

Palmer, R.E. (1969) *Hermeneutics.* Evanston, IL: Northwestern University Press.

Parker, I. (2005) *Qualitative Psychology – Introducing Radical Research.* Buckingham, UK: Open University Press.

Pervin, L.A. (1984) *Personality.* New York: John Wiley.

References

Piaget, J. (1930) *The Child's Conception of the World*. New York: Harcourt, Brace & World.

Plato (1953) *V. Lysis, Symposion, Gorgias* (W.R.M. Lamb, trans.). Cambridge, MA: Harvard University Press.

Poland, B.D. (2002) 'Transcription quality', in J.F. Gubrium and J.A. Holstein (eds), *Handbook of Interview Research*. Thousand Oaks, CA: Sage, pp. 629–49.

Potter, J. and Wetherell, M. (1987) *Discourse and Social Psychology*. London: Sage.

Rapley, T. (2007) *Doing Conversation, Discourse and Document Analysis* (Book 7 of *The SAGE Qualitative Research Kit*). London: Sage.

Richardson, L. and Adams St Pierre, E. (2005) 'Writing: a method of inquiry', in N.K. Denzin and Y.S. Lincoln (eds), *Handbook of Qualitative Research*. Thousand Oaks, CA: Sage, pp. 959–78.

Roethlisberger, F.J. and Dickson, W.J. (1939) *Management and the Worker*. New York: Wiley.

Rogers, C. (1956) *Client-Centered Therapy*. Cambridge, MA: Houghton Mifflin.

Rorty, R. (1979) *Philosophy and the Mirror of Nature*. Princeton, NJ: Princeton University Press.

Rosenau, M.P. (1992) *Postmodernism and the Social Sciences*. Princeton, NJ: Princeton University Press.

Rosenthal, G. (2004) 'Biographical research', in C. Seale, G. Gobo, J.F. Gubrium and D. Silverman (eds), *Qualitative Research Practice*. London: Sage, pp. 48–64.

Rubin, H.J. and Rubin, I.S. (2005) *Qualitative Interviewing*. Thousand Oaks, CA: Sage.

Ryen, A. (2002) 'Cross-cultural interviewing', in J.F. Gubrium and J.A. Holstein (eds), *Handbook of Interview Research*. Thousand Oaks, CA: Sage, pp. 335–54.

Schön, D.A. (1987) *Educating the Reflective Practitioner*. London: Jossey Bass.

Schwandt, T.A. (2001) *Dictionary of Qualitative Inquiry*. Thousand Oaks, CA: Sage.

Seale, C. (2004) 'Quality in qualitative research', in C. Seale, G. Gobo, J.F. Gubrium and D. Silverman (eds), *Qualitative Research Practice*. London: Sage, pp. 407–19.

Seale, C., Gobo. G., Gubrium, J.F. and Silverman, D. (eds) (2004) *Qualitative Research Practice*. London: Sage.

Seidman, I.E. (1991) *Interviewing as Qualitative Research*. New York: Teachers College Press.

Sennett, R. (2004) *Respect*. London: Penguin Books.

Shakespeare, W. (1951) *Collected Works*. London: Collins.

Siegel, S. (1956) *Nonparametric Statistics for the Behavioral Sciences*. New York: McGraw-Hill.

Silverman, D. (2006) *Interpreting Qualitative Data* (3rd ed.). London: Sage.

Silvester, E. (ed.) (1993) *The Penguin Book of Interviews: An Anthology from 1859 to the Present Day*. London: Penguin Books.

Spradley, J. (1979) *The Ethnographic Interview*. New York: Holt, Rinehart & Winston.

Stake, R.E. (2005) 'Case studies', in N.K. Denzin and Y.S. Lincoln (eds), *Handbook of Qualitative Research*. Thousand Oaks, CA: Sage, pp. 443–66.

Strauss, A.M. and Corbin, J. (1990) *Basics of Qualitative Research*. Newbury Park, CA: Sage.

Tanggaard, L. (2007) 'The research interview as discourses crossing swoods', *Qualitative Inquiry*, 13 (1): 160–76.

ten Have, P. (1999) *Doing Conversational Analysis*. Thousand Oaks, CA: Sage.

Tesch, R. (1990) *Qualitative Research: Analysis Types and Software Tools*. London: Falmer.

Tilley, S.A. (2003) 'Transcription work: learning though co-participation in research practices', *Qualitative Studies in Education,* 16: 835–51.

References

Time 100 (1999). New York: Time Books.

van Maanen, J. (1988) *Tales from the Field*. Chicago: Chicago University Press.

Weitzman, E.A. and Miles, M.B. (1995) *Computer Programs for Qualitative Data Analysis*. Thousand Oaks, CA: Sage.

Wengraf, T. (2001) *Qualitative Research Interviewing*. Thousand Oaks, CA: Sage.

Yow, V.R. (1994) *Recording Oral History*. Thousand Oaks, CA: Sage.

▐▐▐ Author index

Adams St Pierre, E., 130
Adorno, T.W., 30, 46
Aristotle, 25–6
Atkinson, P., 7

Bellah, R.N., 31, 75–6, 117, 141, 144

Chrzanowska, J., 47, 72
Comte, A., 21

Denzin, N.K., 7
Derrida, J., 114
Dichter, E., 6

Eder, D., 69
Elster, J., 48

Fog, Jette, 30, 89–90
Foucault, Michel, 112
Freud, Sigmund, 5–6, 18–19, 39, 55, 63, 94, 126, 133

Giorgi, A., 107–8
Glaser, B.G., 6, 38, 105, 123
Gubrium, J.F., 7, 75

Hargreaves, A., 2–3, 39, 117–18, 133, 141
Heidegger, Martin, 49
Hertz, R., 70
Holberg, Ludvig, 136
Holstein, J.A., 7, 75
Huberman, A.M., 116, 123
Husserl, E., 20

Imber, J.B., 70

Janet, P., 6
Jensen, K.B., 110
Jessop, J., 29
Jung, Carl Gustav, 6

Kennedy, M.M., 127
Kerlinger, F.N., 122
Keynes, J.M., 6

Lather, P., 134
Latour, B., 121
Lave, Jean, 40, 48
Lincoln, Y., 7, 25
Lyotard, J.F., 75

Merleau-Ponty, M., 20
Miles, M.B., 99, 116, 123

Ong, W.J., 93

Parker, I., 25, 28
Pervin, L.A., 122
Piaget, Jean, 5–6, 39, 46, 63, 68–79, 88
Plato, 16, 134
Potter, J., 74, 113

Richardson, L., 130
Rogers, Carl, 6, 18, 55, 139
Rorty, Richard, 144

Schön, D.A., 38, 138, 141
Sennett, R., 9, 38, 58, 117, 141
Silverman, D., 7
Smithies, C., 134
Spradley, J., 7
Strauss, A.M., 6, 38, 105, 123

Thucydides, 5
Tilley, S.A., 138

Weitzman, E.A., 99
Wetherell, M., 74, 113

Young, Brigham, 5

III Subject index

action research, 38, 103, 126
active interviews, 75–7, 88
agonistic interviewing, 75, 77
analysis of interview material, 35, 101–19, 121–2
analytical generalization, 127–8, 135
anthropological studies, 5, 20, 40, 52, 71
asymmetry of power between interviewer and interviewee, 14–15, 69–70, 114–15, 121
audiences for interview reports, 129–30, 140

beneficence, principle of, 28
bias, 86–8, 94, 120–3
body language, 93–4
Bourdieu, P., 4, 39, 46, 76, 88, 117–19, 134, 139, 141, 144
bricolage, 115–19
briefing of interview subjects, 55, 65

case studies and case stories, 46, 127, 133
categorization, 105–8
children, interviewing of, 27–8, 68–70
client-centred interviewing, 18, 55
coding, 57, 99, 104–5, 121, 138
communicative validity, 124–8, 135
computers, use of, 7, 19, 98–100, 105
conceptual interviews, 71–2
confidentiality, 24–8, 31
confrontational interviews, 75–7, 88
consumer research, 30, 72
content analysis, 105–6
contextualization, 132–5
conversation, 2, 5, 15, 21, 72, 77
conversation analysis, 111, 114, 132, 143
conversational knowledge, 144–5
criticisms of interview methods, 84–5, 91, 113, 128, 130, 140–1
cultural differences, 67–8, 77, 93

debriefing of interview subjects, 27, 56, 65
deconstruction, 114–15
dialogical interviews, 114–15, 134

dialogical subjectivity and intersubjectivity, 121
discourse analysis, 112–14
discursive interviews, 74–5

elites, interviewing of, 70, 76
emotional dynamics of interviewing, 34–5
empathy, 29–30, 56
ethical guidelines, 25–31
ethical issues, 8–9, 18–19, 23, 28–31, 46, 89–91, 126, 142, 144
experts, interviewing of, 70

field studies, 45–6, 141
Fingerson, L., 69
focus groups, 6, 47, 72, 141
foreign cultures, 67–8, 77
funnel-shaped interviews, 27, 57

generalization from interview studies, 87, 126–7
grounded theory, 38, 105, 123–4

Hamlet, 79–81, 88, 109
hermeneutics, 20, 109, 144
hypothesis-testing, 38, 43–4, 60, 86, 105

informed consent, 24–31, 57
integrity in research, 29–31
interaction between interviewer and interviewee, 13–14, 86, 143
interpretation of meaning, 11–12, 15, 82, 87, 102–9, 114–15, 125, 144
interview(er) questions, 57–65

journalistic methods, 75, 133

knowledge
    construction of, 20–1, 70, 89, 143
    types of, 142–5

leading questions, 69, 87–91, 143
life-world interviews, semistructured, 8, 10–11, 21, 51–3, 65, 71

linguistic analysis, 109–10, 132
linguistic knowledge, 143–4

member validation, 103, 125
metaphor, use of, 116
methodology of interviewing, reporting on, 130–1, 135
micro-ethics of the interview situation, 30–1
'miner' metaphor of interviewing, 19–22, 70, 104, 116, 130, 140
Mishler, E.G., 7, 48–9, 72–3, 95, 97, 112
mixed methods of interview research, 46–8

narrative analysis, 57, 112
narrative interviews, 72–4, 133
non-directive interviewing, 6, 18, 72

objectivity of interview knowledge, 120–2
open questions, 2, 12, 25
oral history, 38, 71, 74
overviews of research, 41–2

participant observation, 45–6
peer validation, 125
planning of interview studies, 33–50
positivism, 20–2, 48, 89, 122
postmodernism, 20–2, 89, 118, 130, 143
pragmatic knowledge, 142–3
pragmatic validation, 126, 128
privacy, protection of, 27–8
psychoanalysis, 47, 49, 94, 109, 141, 144

qualifications for interviewing, 81–3, 91,
qualitative research interviews, 5–9, 11–13, 18, 21–2, 25, 28, 33, 38–9, 43–4, 47–8, 71, 84–9, 109, 121–2, 131, 140–4
    unsuitable subjects for, 45
quality criteria for interviews, 80–1, 84, 90–1, 142
quantitative research, 7, 47, 121

questionnaires, 28, 45–6, 49
quotations from interviews, editing of, 132

reliability of interview knowledge, 113, 122
reporting of research findings, 35, 42, 129–35, 141
research questions, 37, 57–9, 65

science, definitions of, 39, 85–6
scripting of interviews, 56–60
semi-structured interviews, 8, 10–11, 21, 51–3, 57, 65, 71, 74
sensitivity of interviewers, 13, 82, 84
situated knowledge, 143
Socrates and Socratic dialogue, 5, 16, 19, 70, 72, 75–6, 88, 114, 117–18, 134
statistical generalization, 127–8
subcultures, 68
subheadings, use of, 134
subjectivity of research, 86–7, 121–2

tape-recording, 7, 93–4, 111
textual analysis, 98–100, 102, 105
thematization, 35–40
therapeutic interviews, 6, 16–22, 29, 90, 103, 139–40
training of interviewers, 47–9, 139–40
transcription of interviews, 7, 24, 27, 35, 47, 92–102, 111, 132–3, 138–9
translators, use of, 68
'traveller' metaphor of interviewing, 19–22, 70, 89, 104, 116, 129–30, 140

validity of interview knowledge, 87, 122–8
verbatim transcription, 93, 95, 98, 109–10, 132, 134
videotaping of interviews, 94, 141

witness statements, 71, 88, 125
wording of questions, 63, 71, 88